KU-270-242

William Cook

Eric Morecambe Unseen

William Cook

Eric Morecambe Unseen

THE LOST DIARIES JOKES AND PHOTOGRAPHS

Contents

ABOUT THE AUTHOR

WILLIAM COOK is the author of *Ha Bloody Ha* (Fourth Estate), *The Comedy Store* (Little, Brown) and *25 Years of Viz* (Boxtree). He edited *Tragically I Was An Only Twin – The Complete Peter Cook* and *Goodbye Again – The Definitive Peter Cook & Dudley Moore*, both published by Century. He has worked for the BBC and has written for the *Guardian*, the *Mail on Sunday*, the *New Statesman* and *Condé Nast Traveller*.

HarperCollins*Entertainment*
An Imprint of HarperCollins*Publishers*
77–85 Fulham Palace Road,
Hammersmith, London W6 8JB

www.harpercollins.co.uk

Published by HarperCollins*Entertainment* 2005
1

The Author asserts the moral right to
be identified as the author of this work

A CIP catalogue record for this book
is available from the British Library

ISBN 0 00 721222 4

Design by Estuary English

Printed and bound in Great Britain by Butler and Tanner, Frome

Acknowledgements

Grateful thanks to all of the following institutions and individuals for their generous guidance and assistance: the BBC, the British Film Institute, the British Library, The Guardian, Lancaster City Council, Morecambe Library, The Morecambe Visitor, the New Theatre, Oxford; Julian Alexander, Mick and Evelyn Archer, Ronnie Barker, Joel Barnett, Jane Bennett, Eddie Braben, Lucinda Cook, Glen Cooper, Ben Dunn, Bill Drysdale, Mike and Leslie Fountain, Bill Franklyn, Kate Latham, Tony Lyons, Francis Matthews, Gail Morecambe, Steven Morecambe, Jo O'Callaghan, Rachel Nicholson, Val Pozzoli, David Secombe, Jim Trotman, Peter Wade, Lynn Wilman and Cy Young. And above all, a very big thank you to Joan and Gary Morecambe, without whom this book never could have been compiled, let alone published. Fame often casts a long shadow over the lives of great entertainers, and their families – but Eric Morecambe's life, though far too brief, was almost always sunny. Thanks to the discreet yet heartfelt efforts of his family, some of that sunshine has survived.

Chapter 1

HARPENDEN

Ernie: What's the matter with you?
Eric: I'm an idiot. What's your excuse?

AT FIRST GLANCE, the house doesn't look like much – not from the main road, at least. It's detached but fairly modern, built of unpretentious brick. The front lawn is neat but nondescript. Most of the garden is around the back. There's a friendly Alsatian dozing in the drive. She sits up but doesn't bark. There's an outdoor swimming pool, but it's purely functional, not fancy. In fact, the most remarkable thing about this house is that there's nothing remarkable about it. It's a place you'd be pleased to live in, but it's hardly the sort of place you'd associate with one of the greatest comedians who ever lived.

Eric Morecambe's house in smart, respectable, suburban Harpenden is a lot like the brilliant comic we all knew – or thought we knew – and loved. From the moment you arrive, it feels strangely familiar. Even on your first visit, it seems like somewhere you've been coming all your life. 'It wasn't a show business house,' says Eric's old chauffeur, Mike Fountain, who comes from Harpenden. 'It was a family home.' And it still is. Like Eric, it feels safe and comforting, without the slightest hint of ostentation. And from 1968 until his untimely death in 1984, it was the home of a man who, more than anyone, summed up the Great British sense of humour.

Britain has always been blessed with more than its fair share of comedians, but there's never been another comic we've taken so completely to our hearts. Peter Cook, Peter Sellers, Tony Hancock, Spike Milligan – these were comics we adored, but there was always something remote, almost otherworldly, about them. We laughed at them rather than with them. Sure, we found them funny – but secretly, we thought they were rather strange. Eric Morecambe was awfully funny, but there was nothing remotely strange about him. To millions like me, who never knew him, he was like a favourite uncle, with a unique gift for making strangers laugh like old friends.

More than twenty years after he died, from a heart attack, aged just 58, Eric's irrepressible personality still lingers in every corner of his comfortable home. There's a framed photograph on the piano of him hobnobbing with the Queen Mother, and for a moment you wonder how on earth Eric, our Eric, got to meet the Queen Mum. But then you see a photo of Ernie Wise alongside it, and you remember. He wasn't our Eric at all – that was his great illusion – but half of Britain's finest, funniest double act, Morecambe & Wise.

From the 1960s to the 1980s, Morecambe & Wise were the undisputed heavyweight champions of British comedy. Christmas was inconceivable without their TV special. Their fans ranged from members of the Royal Family to members of the KGB. Their humour was timeless and classless, and that was what made them irresistible. They were stylish yet childlike, and they united the nation unlike any other act, before or since. You could laugh at Eric if you were seven. You could laugh at him if you were seventy. Old or young, rich or poor, you couldn't fail to find him funny. He didn't seem like a celebrity. He felt like one of the family, which is why it feels so normal to be standing here, in the cosy house where he used to live. Eric once said he wanted daily life here to be as average as possible, and funnily enough, it still is. 'The overwhelming impression I formed of Eric,' says his old friend Sue Nicholls, better known to the rest of us as Audrey in Coronation Street, 'is just how ordinary he was.'[1] Yet this ordinary

man had an extraordinary talent, and the most extraordinary part of it is how ordinary he made it seem. As his wife, Joan, says, with simple clarity, 'He was one of them.'

Joan still lives here, just like she used to live here with Eric. She's never remarried, and she has no plans to move. She still wears his ring, and she still thinks of him as her husband. She sometimes refers to him in the present tense, as if he's still around. After all these years, she still half expects to see him pop his head around the door. 'To me it always seems as if Eric's only just gone,' she tells me. 'It never seems to me that it's been twenty years.' Yet after today, there will be slightly less of Eric here than there was before. After twenty years, she's been clearing out her husband's study – a room that had lain dormant since he died. There was all sorts of stuff in there – photos, letters, joke books, diaries. It sounded as if there might be a book in it. 'You can't explain it,' says Joan. 'You can't explain why people still remember him as if he's still part of their lives.' She's probably right. You can never really explain these things – not definitively, not completely. But once I've spent a few hours inside Eric's study, I reckon I'll have a much better idea.

We go upstairs, past his full length portrait in the stairwell, and into a small room – barely more than a box room, really – where Eric would retreat to read and write. There's a lovely view out the back, across the golf course and over open fields beyond, where Eric would go golfing or bird watching. He quite liked a round of golf, but on the whole he far preferred birds to birdies. He loved to watch them fly by, especially when he was resting.

However there's nothing restful about this room, despite its peaceful vistas. This was where Eric came to work, not just to rest or play. 'This book laden room was his shrine,' observed Gary, just a few days after his father's death. 'Almost every previous time I had entered it, I had discovered his hunched figure poised over his portable typewriter, the whole room engulfed with smoke from his meerschaum pipe.'[2] Two decades on, that same sense of restless industry endures. It may be twenty years, but it feels like Eric has just nipped out for an ounce of pipe tobacco. It feels like he'll be back any minute. It feels as if we're trespassing in a comedic Tutankhamen's tomb.

On the floor beside the bookcase is an old biscuit tin. Inside is his passport, his ration book and his Luton Town season ticket. There's a shoe box full of old pipes, with blackened bowls and well chewed stems. Here's his hospital tag, made out in his real name, John Bartholomew, so he wouldn't be pestered by starstruck patients. On the back of the door is his velvet smoking jacket – black and crimson, like a prop from one of Ernie's dreadful plays. 'He loved dressing in a Noel Coward kind of way,' says Gary, vaguely, his thoughts elsewhere. But it's the books on the shelves above that really catch your eye. Never mind Desert Island Discs. For the uninvited visitor, there's nothing quite so intimate as someone else's library. When you scan another person's bookshelves, it's as if you're browsing in the corridors of their mind.

As you might expect, there are stacks of joke books: Laughter, The Best Medicine; The Complete Book of Insults; Twenty Thousand Quips And Quotes. And as you might expect, there are stacks of books about other jokers, many of them American, from silent clowns like Buster Keaton to wise guys like Groucho Marx. Yet it's the less likely titles that reveal most about Britain's favourite joker: PG Wodehouse, Richmal Crompton, even the Kama Sutra. And here's Charles Dickens' The Pickwick Papers, 'Eric always told me that The Pickwick Papers was the funniest book he had ever read,' says Gary. 'He used to read it on train journeys when he was travelling from theatre to theatre, from digs to digs. He said he'd get strange looks from the people in his carriage, because he was stifling his laughter as he read.' There's Tom Stoppard's Rosencrantz & Guildenstern Are Dead. There's a bit of Eric in all these books – well, maybe not the Kama Sutra. Wodehouse? Certainly. Dickens? Of course. Eric and Ernie would have been brilliant as Rosencrantz and Guildenstern, but the character Eric most resembles is Crompton's Just William, an eternal eleven year old with a genius

Eric wasn't just a pipe smoker, he was a pipe collector too. He owned several hundred pipes. This one, which he called his Sherlock Holmes pipe, was a particular favourite

Mr and Mrs Eric Morecambe

Ernie: 'I can see your lips moving. Eric: Well of course you can, you flaming fool! I'm the one who's doing it for him! He's made of wood! His mother was a Pole!' Right to left: Ernie, Eric and Charlie the Dummy, who still resides at the Morecambe residence in Harpenden, awaiting repairs.

for amiable mischief. 'Maybe that's why we loved him as kids,' says Gary's lifelong friend, Bill Drysdale, a regular visitor to this house ever since he was a child. 'The thing that kids love more than anything is the idea of grown ups being naughty. Kids think that's just the funniest thing, and that's what I always loved about him.'

As a child, Bill wasn't remotely awestruck by Eric's stardom. 'I never felt alienated by his status,' he says. 'You always felt like he was one of us.' Yet he was full of surprises. After Eric died, Bill found a Frank Zappa album, of all things, in Eric's record collection. 'There was often the appearance of anarchy, but there was one person at the centre of things who knew exactly what was going on,' says Bill, of Zappa's music, 'and that is an ideal template, I think, for Eric's comedy.' Eric's comedy wasn't just a job. It was a way of life. 'His mind was always working on comedy,' says Bill. 'He'd be working in the study, he'd come out and he'd try out a joke on Gary and I, just to see what we thought of it, to see if it was funny.' He knew if children found it funny, it would be easy to make their parents laugh.

We walk down the narrow corridor, to Eric's old bedroom. The overflow from his study is strewn across the floor. There's the giant lollipop which was his trademark before he met Ernie – a twelve year old vaudevillian, kitted out in beret and bootlace tie.[3] Here's a clapperboard from The Intelligence Men, the first feature film he made with Ernie. And there's the ventriloquist's dummy that was the highlight of their live show. 'I can see your lips moving,' Ernie would protest each time, in immaculate mock indignation. 'Well of course you flaming can, you fool!' Eric would answer, furious at this outrageous slur on his professional integrity. 'I'm the one who's doing it for him!' He's made of wood! His mother was a Pole!' 'He had the common touch,' says Gary. 'He wasn't trying to be hip or clever.' But that was another part of Eric's artifice. Eric did what all great artists do. He made it look easy.

There are heaps of photos all around us, some dating back to Eric and Ernie's first turns together, as teenagers during the war. With his boyish good looks and eager grin, Ernie looks just the same as he always did. Eric, on the other hand, is almost unrecognisable – painfully thin and curiously feminine, with high cheekbones and a full head of dark, wavy hair. There are piles of cuttings too, newspaper after newspaper – countless rave reviews, even the occasional stinker. So important at the time, or so it seemed. All forgotten now, of course. As Eric used to say, to buck himself up after a bad notice, or bring himself back down to earth after a good one, the hardest thing to find is yesterday's paper. And here they all are – all his daily papers from all his yesteryears. There are endless interviews, in every publication you can think of (and quite a few you can't) from a profile by Kenneth Tynan in The Observer to a cover story in that classic boy's comic, Tiger. Today these faded clippings all seem incongruously similar. Highbrow or lowbrow, they're all mementoes of a life lived almost entirely in the public gaze.

This is a book about the part the public didn't see. In the wings, in the dressing room, at home or on holiday, Eric Morecambe had a compulsion to amuse. 'Even if he didn't have an audience or wasn't getting paid, he'd still entertain people in his kitchen,' says Gary. 'He used to wake up thinking funny. It was almost like an illness.' Unlike a lot of comics, he didn't hoard his humour for his paying punters. He was always on.

Some of it ended up on the small screen, where the rest of us could relish it. Some of it vanished into thin air. And the rest is in this room. Here's his address book – a veritable Who's Who of the glory days of British showbiz: Ronnie Barker, Roy Castle, Tommy Cooper and Harry Secombe. There's a number for Des O'Connor, the patient butt of so many put downs, plus sporting pals like Dickie Davies and Jimmy Hill. There are numbers for his writer, Eddie Braben, his producer, John Ammonds, and, naturally, Ernie Wise – plus the British Heart Foundation, an association that ended with his third and final, fatal heart attack, bringing their lifelong partnership to an abrupt and inconclusive end. 'Eric Morecambe' reads Eric's own inscription on the inside cover. 'Comedian – Retired.' But Eric never hung up his boots. He worked until the day – the very evening – that he died.

There are other books in this cardboard box, but they're not address books. They're notebooks filled with jottings, from diary entries to old jokes. Some, in childlike copperplate, date back half a century. Others, in geriatric scrawl, look like they were scribbled down yesterday. But buried in amongst these reflections, reminiscences and corny old one-liners, two quotations arrest the eye. One is by TS Eliot, from The Love Song of J Alfred Prufrock: 'I grow old, I grow old, I shall wear the bottoms of my trousers rolled.'[4] The other must be from the Gospel of St. John, which is odd, since Eric wasn't overtly religious: 'That which was borne of this flesh is flesh – that which was borne of the spirit is spirit.' Well, the flesh is gone – long gone – but in those photos and notebooks, and in this book, the daft, endearing spirit of Eric Morecambe lives on. 'Even when he wasn't here, it was as if this place was echoing with his infectious laugh,' says Bill Drysdale. This book is all about the echo of that laughter.

Top: **My other car is a Rolls** Bottom: **My other car is a Skoda**

Eric and Fiona Castle (Roy Castle's wife) take each other's photos

Eric, Joan and their daughter, Gail, along with additional family members Barney, the Retriever, and Chips.

Top: **Eric relaxing at Elbow Beach Hotel in Bermuda, on the way home from appearing on the Ed Sullivan Show in New York.**

Below: **Gail points out her first boyfriend to her father.**

Top: **Gail and Gary with Eric and Joan in the garden of their home in Harpenden, just after Gail's confirmation.**

Left: **Eric with his mother in law, Alice**

Above: Eric relaxes by the family pool with wife Joan and children Gail and Gary. In fact, Eric couldn't swim and never once went in the water.

Right: 1969, the day Apollo 11 got back, carved by Eric, with his initials, on a tree in his front garden.

Above: **Chez Eric. Left to right: Gail, Joan, Eric and Gary.**

Below: **A new addition to the family: Joan and Eric's adopted son, Steven.**

Eric and Ernie – tears of a clown.

Chapter 2
MORECAMBE

Eric: I'm not a complete fool.
Ernie: Why? What part's missing?

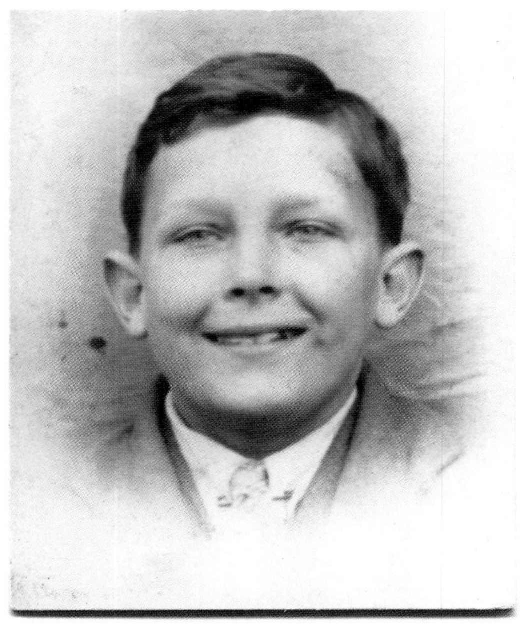

EVEN THE CIRCUMSTANCES of Eric's birth were vaguely comical. He was born John Eric Bartholomew on 14 May 1926, at 42 Buxton Road, Morecambe, but his mother and father actually lived a few doors away. They'd had to move in with neighbours while their own house was repaired. Once their proper home was patched up they moved back in again, but within a year it had become unfit for human habitation. Eric's earliest memory was the ceiling collapsing. It must have been pretty awful at the time, of course, especially for his hard pressed parents, but looking back it sounds like a slapstick scene from one of his favourite silent films.

Above: **'I'm not saying his ears were big, but when you saw him from the front, he looked like the FA Cup.' Eric, before his mother Sadie started taping back his ears, to stop them sticking out.**

Although he was already taking dancing lessons, and entering local talent contests, Eric's boyhood dream was to become a professional footballer. And unlike most of his teammates, this was no idle fantasy. A fine left winger, he attracted the interest of several league scouts, but his father, who'd suffered a crippling injury as an amateur, advised him against it. In those days there was no money in it, and your career was over by the time you were thirty, so Eric subsequently decided it would be a better bet to settle for show business instead.

Buxton Road is the sort of terraced street you see in Lowry paintings, full of kids playing football, but by the time Eric was old enough to kick a ball his parents had moved into a new council house, 43 Christie Avenue, behind the main stand of Morecambe Football Club, where Eric lived until he left home. By modern standards, Eric's childhood home in Christie Avenue looks pretty Spartan, but back in the 1920s it was a proletarian dream come true. It had three bedrooms, its own front door, and best of all, its own garden – still a rarity in those days, especially for folk of the Bartholomew's humble social standing. This garden was the summit of Eric's father's expectations. Luckily for Eric, and the future of British comedy, his mother's aspirations weren't confined to this pleasant but unprepossessing patch of lawn.

Eric's parents both came from similar working class backgrounds, but their personalities could hardly have been less alike. Orphaned at an early age, his mother Sadie was a sharp and restless woman who was always striving to better herself – and her family. His father George, on the other hand, was one of those rare individuals who are utterly contented with their lot. One of life's plodders, he toiled away serenely as

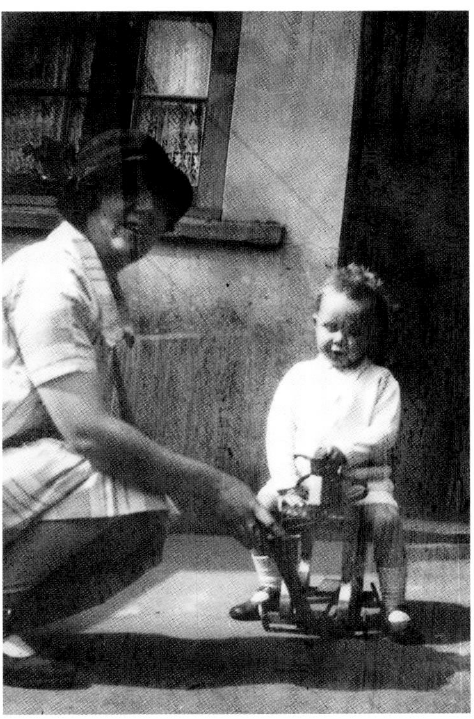

Above: **Some of the earliest photos of Eric with his mother, Sadie.** Below: **The future Mr Eric Morecambe, OBE.**

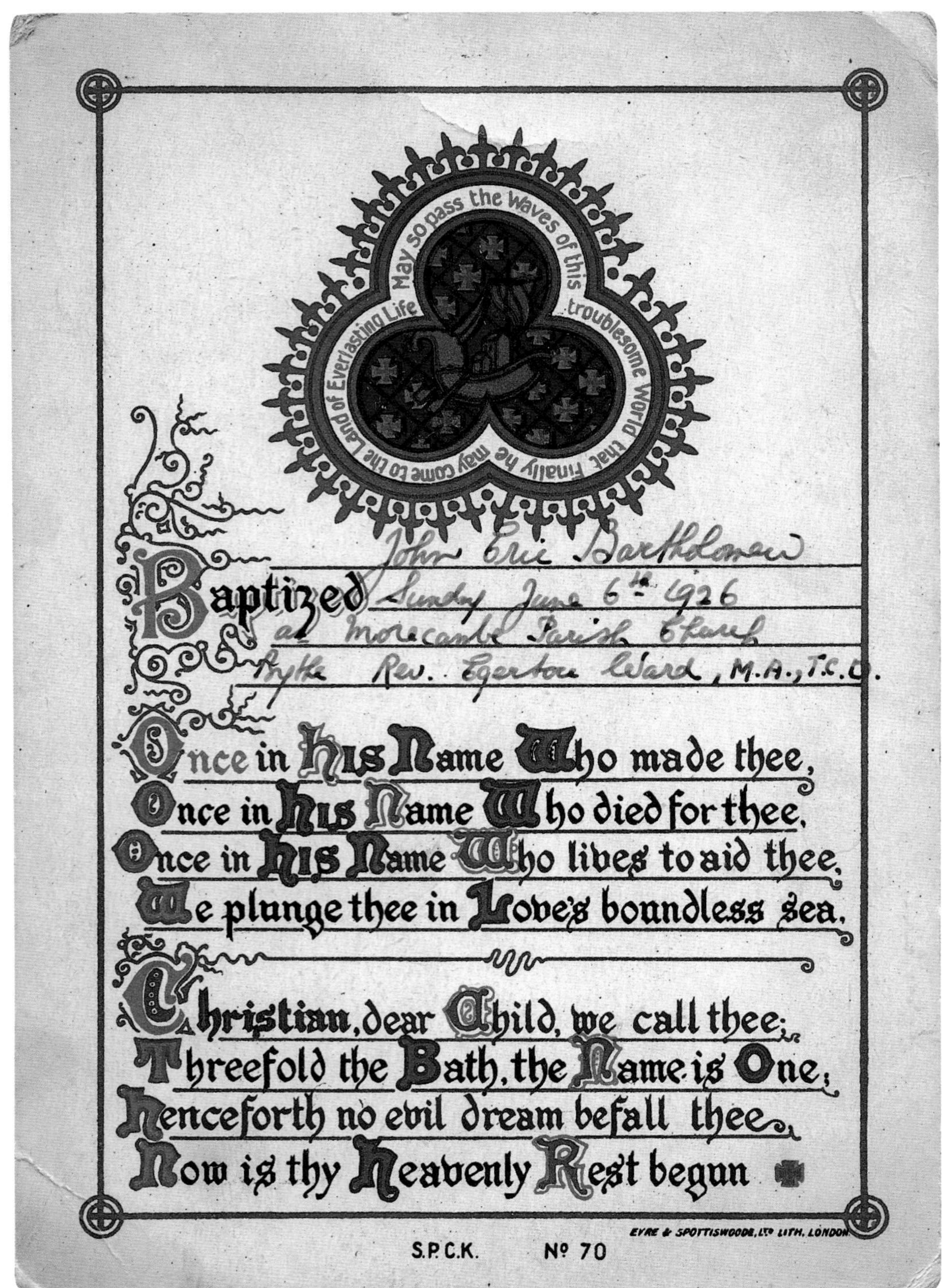
May so pass the waves of this troublesome World that finally he may come to the Land of Everlasting Life
John Eric Bartholomew
Baptized Sunday June 6th 1926
at Morecambe Parish Church
by the Rev. Egerton Ward, M.A., T.C.D.
Once in His Name Who made thee,
Once in His Name Who died for thee,
Once in His Name Who lives to aid thee,
We plunge thee in Love's boundless sea.
Christian, dear Child, we call thee;
Threefold the Bath, the Name is One;
Henceforth no evil dream befall thee,
Now is thy Heavenly Rest begun
EYRE & SPOTTISWOODE, LTD LITH. LONDON
S.P.C.K. Nº 70

Lancaster Road Junior School, Morecambe. Eric is second from the left on the front row.

a council labourer from the day he left school until the day he retired, entirely satisfied with the modest cards he'd been dealt. Like the soldier in the wartime song, he really did whistle while he worked. Despite their contrasting attitudes – or perhaps, in part, because of them – George and Sadie got along very well. In their very different ways, they each nurtured Eric, and he formed a close bond with both of them that would sustain him throughout his life. Eric's incredible career was a testament to his driven (and hard driving) mother, but his happy go lucky stage persona was a tribute to his easy going dad. 'George was a character,' says his grandson, Gary. 'I remember giving him some aftershave for Christmas, and him ringing up and saying it was the worst sherry he'd ever drunk.' It sounds like a classic Eric Morecambe one liner.

In many ways, Eric's was a typical working class childhood. His parents were far from affluent (when they went shopping in Lancaster, several miles away, they used to walk home to save the bus fare) but Eric never went hungry. And though money was often pretty tight, he never ran short of fun things to do. On Sundays George would take him fishing, and on Saturdays they'd go to a football match – usually Morecambe, sometimes Blackpool, occasionally mighty Preston North End. Yet there was one

MORECAMBE AND HEYSHAM EDUCATION COMMITTEE

EUSTON ROAD SENIOR SCHOOL.

SCHOLAR'S REPORT for Half Year ending February 1939

Name John E Bartholomew

Age 12 yrs 9 mths Class ~~or Group~~ E (II C)

Average Age of Class ~~or Group~~ 12 yrs 11 mths

Number of Scholars in Class ~~or Group~~ 38

Times Absent 2 Times Late 0

Conduct Good.

Subject	Marks possible	Marks gained	Position	Out of	Remarks
Mathematics	50	18	9	36	
English	60	47	5	37	
Geography	20	14	2	32	With a little more care,
History	20	13	9	37	
Science	20	10½	10	29	Eric could be one of the
Practical Drawing	10	5	16	18	
Object Drawing	10	2	11	19	best scholars. If he
Needlework	–				
Craft Work	20	8	36	38	concentrates on Mathematics
Woodwork or Cookery	20	10	8	19	
Music	–				drawing and General neatness
Handwriting	20	13	8	37	
					he will have better results
Neatness	20	9	33	38	next Term. I think he can
Other Tests	80	49	6	38	do it.
Totals & Final Position	350	198½	10	38	

Signature of Headmaster R W Sporne

Signature of Class Master ~~or Mistress~~ A. C. Lamb.

Signature of Parent or Guardian G. Bartholomew

School re-opens on 17th April 1939

MORECAMBE AND HEYSHAM EDUCATION COMMITTEE.

LANCASTER ROAD COUNCIL SCHOOL

SCHOLAR'S REPORT.

Pupil's Name Bartholomew Eric

Class Grade III Term ending 9th April 1936

Position in Class 45 out of 49

Average age of class 9 years 6 months

Times absent 20 Times late — for period ending 31st Mar

Conduct Good Games Good

SUBJECTS	MARKS POSSIBLE	MARKS GAINED	TEACHER'S REMARKS
Reading	20	13	
Recitation	10	·	
Grammar	10	·	
Composition	20	6a	He was absent
Spelling	10	7	most of the exams.
Penmanship	10	3	
Arithmetic	40	10	
Mental Arithmetic	20	6	
Geography	20	·	
History	20	·	
Science	20	·	
Drawing	20	10	
Brush-Drawing (B) / Needlework (G)	20	·	
Total	240	55	

R Burgin Class Teacher

C. T. Brannes. Head Master.

Signature of Parent (or Guardian) S. Bartholomew

aspect of his upbringing that was highly unusual, at least for those days. He was an only child. This oddity was to prove crucial for his future prospects. Had he been one of six children, like his mother, or one of eleven, like his father, it's highly unlikely he would have been able to pursue the same show business career.

However despite a happy and comparatively comfortable home life, Eric did surprisingly badly at school. 'I wasn't just hopeless in class,' he recalled. 'I was terrible.'[1] His school reports bear him out. Out of a class of 49, he was ranked 45 – and the other four, according to Eric, never even went to school. Eric's poor academic performance remains a mystery, especially since Sadie was not only intelligent, but diligent too. 'I am disgusted with this report,' she wrote to his headmaster, 'and would be obliged if you would make him do more homework.' Her efforts were in vain. When Sadie told the head she wanted Eric to go to grammar school, he told her it would be a waste of time. When she said she'd pay for private education, he said it would be money down the drain. For the time being, at least, Eric was his father's son. 'I had no bright ambitions,' he recollected. 'To me, my future was clear. At fifteen I would get myself a paper round. At seventeen I would learn to read it. And at eighteen I would get a job on the Corporation, like my dad.'[2]

If there was one thing Eric was good at, it was performing. Ever since he was a toddler, he'd entertained his parents by dancing to the gramophone. Once, he sneaked out of the house and onto a nearby building site, where Sadie found him treating local workmen to a song and dance routine. 'That little lad's a wonderful entertainer,'[3] said one of them. 'I'll entertain him when I get home,'[4] said Sadie, yet she did all she could to nurture her son's nascent talent. Egged on by his mum, Eric studied half a dozen musical instruments, including the piano and the accordion, and although he never mastered any of them, it didn't do his sense of rhythm any harm. He cultivated his showbiz education at the local cinema, although his interest in the movies came second to his interest in making mischief. On at least one occasion, he was thrown out for firing his pea shooter at the heads of bald men in the stalls.

Sadie also sent Eric to dancing classes, and when the teacher recommended individual lessons, at a cost of two and six a time, she toiled as a charlady to pay for them, on top of her day job as an usherette on Morecambe Central Pier. To make a few extra bob, she'd gather up the discarded programmes, bring them home, iron them until they looked brand new, and resell them at the theatre the next day. Despite her sacrifices, Eric was far from keen. 'I never liked the lessons,' he recalled. 'I'd have much preferred to have spent my time kicking a ball around with my mates.'[5] Yet Sadie's

Left: **The Bash Street Kids. Eric is in the middle of the front row. 'I was just a shy, bashful sort of boy. Why, even when I was six I used to blush every time I hit a policeman.'**

Below: **Unwillingly to school. A reluctant Eric sets off for Lancaster Road Junior School, where he reached the dizzy heights of 45th out of a class of 49.**

investment soon paid off. Before long, he was playing local working men's clubs, often for as much as fifteen shillings a time – half his father's weekly wage.

As a budding entertainer, Eric was lucky to be the only child of such a shrewd and dedicated mother, but he was also lucky to born in the right place at the right time. Today Morecambe is a quiet resort on the edge of the Lake District, frequented mainly by flocks of wading birds and the birdwatchers that come to watch them, but in the 1930s, when Eric was a lad, it was a thriving holiday town. Smarter than nearby

Eric's dad George (far right) with his workmates from Morecambe Corporation. A world away from the Morecambe & Wise Show.

Blackpool, but with much of the same seaside bustle, it was a lively place of entertainment, whose shows spilled out of the dancehalls and onto the promenade. Eric's mum and dad met at the Winter Gardens, a splendid ballroom where Eric would later perform with Ernie. Full of precocious self confidence, he entered talent contests on the prom, winning so often that locals were eventually barred from competing, since his success was discouraging genuine holidaymakers from joining in.

Fortunately, such competitions weren't confined to Morecambe promenade, and Sadie soon found a bigger stage for her prodigious child. After several decent write ups in the local press, he finally got his big break in 1939 when he won a juvenile talent show in Hoylake, a seaside town on the Wirral. For Eric, it felt like travelling to Australia, but this odyssey was well worthwhile. 'Eric Bartholomew put over a brilliant comedy act which caused the audience to roar with laughter,' reported the Melody Maker, the show's sponsor, and their interview with Eric revealed another side to the lad who'd been content to drift through school. 'My ambition is to be a comedian,' Eric told the paper. 'My hero is George Formby.' In later life, Eric confessed that he actually

Eric's mum and dad, George and Sadie, all set to emigrate to America, with George's brother, Jack, and Jack's wife, Alice. They'd even bought their tickets, but then Jack fell ill, and they all got cold feet. Just think: if Jack hadn't been poorly, Eric would have grown up in America. Would he have become the next Bob Hope? Or merely the next John Bartholomew?

Eric with his mum and dad, George and Sadie, in their Sunday best.

found Formby 'about as funny as a cry for help,'[6] but it was telling that his role model was one of the best known (and best paid) comics in the country. His dad's laid back approach, which informed Eric's lackadaisical school career, had been eclipsed by his mum's determination and drive.

Eric's prize was yet another audition, but this try out was a cut above the usual talent show. This time, he'd won an audience with Jack Hylton, one of the top impresarios in the land. The audition was held in Manchester, another epic journey for Eric. Sadie couldn't stand those showbiz mums who sought glory through the (real or imagined) talents of their children. Nevertheless, she was determined to get Eric's head out of the clouds and – if at all possible – improve his prospects. Hence, she left him in no doubt about the significance of this trip. 'She drummed into me all the way from Morecambe that this just might be the most important day of my life,' recalled Eric. 'And she was right.'[7] For sitting in the stalls, in pride of place alongside Hylton, was an accomplished young entertainer called Ernie Wise.

*

Eric in his talent contest days.

Above: **A dapper, dashing young Eric poses for his public alongside a female admirer (his Auntie Alice).**

Right: **Master Eric Bartholomew, Vocal Comedy & Dancing Act.**

Above: **Eric's mum and dad, George and Sadie.**

Below: **George and Sadie celebrate their golden wedding anniversary with their only son.**

Chapter 3

BARTHOLOMEW & WISEMAN

Eric: Do you remember our first meeting?

Ernie: Yes, I do remember. We decided to team up and have a go at comedy.

Eric: We should have tried that.

For a lad of thirteen, Eric Bartholomew had already come a long way – but compared to Ernie Wise, he was still an untried amateur. Eric, at that time, was just another wannabe. Ernie, on the other hand, was already a bona fide star. He'd been on the BBC, appeared in a West End show and received rave reviews in the national newspapers. He was six months older than Eric. It might as well have been six years.

Ernest Wiseman was born in Leeds on 27 November 1925. His father, Harry, had been decorated for bravery during the First World War, but like a lot of war heroes, he didn't take too well to peacetime. He worked on the railways in a variety of fairly menial occupations, but his meagre wages did nothing to quell his extravagant nature. He met Ernie's mother, Connie, on a local tram. It was love at first sight. Connie's father thought Harry was far too common for his daughter, and threatened to cut her off without a penny if she married him. He was a man of his word. When Connie and Harry got married and moved into a rented room together, the only thing she was allowed to take with her was the piano she'd saved up to buy.

Ernie was the first of five children, and Connie had to be incredibly careful and resourceful to feed a family of seven on just a couple of pounds a week. From his mum, Ernie learnt that your bank book is your best friend, a motto which stood him in good stead as the business brains behind Britain's most successful comic duo. In the years to come, Eric would make countless quips about Ernie's cautious attitude to money. Like all the best jokes, this running gag was based on painful experience. Long after he became a wealthy man, with more cash than he could ever hope to spend, Ernie would still maintain that the main thing in life is being able to pay your bills.

Thankfully for everyone concerned (except, perhaps, Connie's father) Harry's paltry salary was supplemented – and then rapidly superseded – when Ernie joined his dad onstage. Harry was already a part time performer on the local working men's club circuit, but his act really took off when he teamed up with Ernie, who'd shown similar showbiz flair as Eric from a similarly early age. 'I'd come on and do a clog dance and members of the audience used to throw pennies,' he recalled.[1] Still only seven years old, he found it hard to stay awake at school, but performing trumped anything the classroom had to offer. Soon Carson & Kid, as they called themselves, were earning several pounds every weekend – more than Harry earned in a whole week on the railway. By the time Ernie played the Bradford Alhambra, aged eleven, in the Nignog Revue (political correctness had yet to be invented) he was already a veteran. Now called Bert Carson & His Little Wonder, Harry and Ernie were fast becoming the toast of the Yorkshire halls.

Above, right and overleaf: **I'm not all there... Eric's first professional act, showing off the results of all those song and dance lessons that his mother made him undergo in Morecambe.**

It's tantalising to wonder whether Harry and Ernie could have gone on to even greater things, but their partnership ended in 1938 when a man called Bryan Michie came to town. Michie was scouring the country for fresh talent for Jack Hylton's latest juvenile revue, and when he saw Ernie do a turn at the Leeds Empire, he sent him straight down to London so Hylton could see this Little Wonder for himself. Hylton was so impressed, he put Ernie in a West End show that very evening. The show was Band Waggon, starring Arthur Askey, but it was Ernie who was singled out for special praise in the overnight reviews. 'His timing and confidence are remarkable,' raved the Daily Express. 'At thirteen he is an old time performer.'[2] His surname shortened to Wise, at Hylton's instigation, when Eric first set eyes on him, in Manchester in 1939, he'd already matured into a seasoned pro.

Eric was still raw compared to Ernie, but there was no mistaking his talent. 'Go out there and give them all you've got,' Sadie told him, as they waited in the wings. 'If you pull it off I'll buy you an airgun.'[3] Eric gave it both barrels. Ernie spotted Eric's star

1939.

GAY SPARKS OF THE ELECTRICITY DEPT.

A JOLLY SOCIAL.

Informality was the keynote of a gathering held in the Elms Hotel on Saturday evening by the Corporation Electricity Dept. Social Club. The jolly atmosphere made a great success of the games and dancing.

Merry-maker-in-chief was the Borough Electrical Engineer, Mr. Percy Clegg, who was M.C. There were no wall-flowers for he made everyone join in the fun.

The event was organised jointly by the ladies' committee, under the chairmanship of Mrs. Clegg, and the men's committee under Chairman R. Woodhouse.

Eric Bartholomew, the boy entertainer, scored with such songs as "Kiss Me Goodnight, Sergeant Major" and "There'll be flats where the arches used to be." Mr. Dick (T.N.T.) Taylor, assisted by Mr. Joe Turpin, the property horse, caused hilarity with his illustration of "How to sell a thoroughbred." Songs were sung by Mr. J. Smith (baritone) and Miss Joan Woodhouse (contralto). Musical items were provided by Mr. Ernest Berry (pianist) and the Accordian Trio.

An excellent dinner, in keeping with the reputation of the Elms' management, was served by Mr. A. Beck and his staff.

Like the grown-ups' social the children's Christmas party in the afternoon was a great success. A Mickey Mouse cinema show by Mr. Wm. Brown was greatly enjoyed. Eric Bartholomew made as big a hit with the youngsters as he did with their parents. In addition to party games, several of the older boys and girls sang solos and Mr. Lewis Keighley played the piano.

Father Christmas (Dick Taylor) gave sticks of T.N.T., an orange and an apple to more than 100 children.

1939

BOY WITH A FUTURE.

MAKES HIT IN SOLDIERS' SHOW.

Biggest hit in the variety interlude by soldiers at the Odeon cinema's sixth military night on Friday was made by a 13 years old Morecambe boy, Eric Bartholomew.

Odeon manager Mr. J. V. Sanders, in voicing thanks to the artistes, prophesied that the boy would go far in a stage career. By their applause, the audience showed they agreed.

In song, comedy and dance, Eric scored all along the line. There was not a trace of nervousness about him as he put over his numbers, which included the topical "Kiss Me Good-night, Sergeant Major."

Corpl Staunton mingled a host of amusing stories with comic songs. Crooning and straight singing were provided by Ptes Taylor, Perry and Arnold, whose solos included "South of the Border" and "Penny Serenade"—tunes in which the audience joined heartily.

The usual community singing went with a swing, Mr. Ivor Gladwin playing a piano-accordian accompaniment. Mr. Gladwin also accompanied the artistes. Mr. Sanders voiced special thanks to him for standing by on each of the military nights in case his services were needed.

1939.

BOY VOLUNTEER MAKES A HIT.

Two soldiers, and a boy from the audience, who volunteered to sing, filled the breach in the Odeon military night variety interlude on Friday, when duty prevented several soldier artistes from attending.

Lance Corporal Whelan got a great reception for his tenor solos, and Private Barber, a clever guitarist, brought the house down with his impersonation of Nat Gonella.

Soldiers in the audience were invited to "do their stuff" on the stage but they were all too shy. Then a young boy from the audience saved the situation. He sang several songs including "Kiss Me Sergeant Major," and "Music, Maestro, Please." He was repeatedly encored.

Next Friday, Bandmaster Brown and his boys from the King's Own will give a completely new programme. Patrons are asked to note that the last complete round begins at 6-25.

1939

TALENT-SPOTTING COMPETITION

Morecambe Boy First

A SHOW within a show was staged at the Arcadian Theatre on Saturday night when the final of the talent-spotting competition took place.

The standard of local talent was surprisingly high and the audience enjoyed it immensely. It was only after considerable difficulty that Peter Bernard, one of the artistes in the variety show, was able to select the three winners, who were chosen by the applause the audience gave them.

First prize was won by the Morecambe boy, Eric Bartholomew, whose singing of "I'm Not All There" really got the crowd. Pte Waters, who looked and sang like Bing Crosby, was a good second. He sang "Somewhere In France." Harry Ward, a hiking comedian, brought the house down for the third award.

Other competitors were: Miss Bessie Douglas, Ronald Redfern, Pte. MacNulty, Dot Bennett, Alf Peacock, Peggy Ellison, Troughton Bros. and Two Guitars, Diana Copeland and The Three Crack-Pots.

1939.

ONE OUT OF 100.

MOREFAMBE BOY TO GO FOR LONDON AUDITION.

THIRTEEN-YEARS-OLD Eric Bartholomew, the well known local juvenile stage artiste, who has made such hits in local entertainments, has gone a step further in his career, for he has been chosen as one of the four finalists for the Lancashire and Cheshire area in the search-for-talent competition organised by the journal "Melody Maker."

The competition is linked up with Jack Hylton's radio and stage feature, "Youth Takes a Bow." The finalists in the area competition will travel to London for special auditions before Jack Hylton.

Young Bartholomew was one of ten competitors who succeeded in reaching the area final for Lancashire and Cheshire. There were one hunderd competitors in the area. The ten finalists appeared at the Kingsway Cinema, Hoylake, a week ago, when Eric was chosen with three others to travel to London. The other three were all girls from Liverpool.

"A BRILLIANT COMEDIAN ACT."

The "Melody Maker" report of the area final states:

"**Eric Bartholomew put over a brilliant comedian act which caused the audience to roar with laughter.**

'In an interview, he said 'My ambition is to become a comedian. My hero is George Formby, another native of Lancashire. I would certainly like to follow in his footsteps.'"

Eric won a talent-spotting competition at Morecambe Arcadian Theatre last month.

No. 807

12	18	25	36	50	75	100
7/6	10/-	12/6	17/6	22/6	32/6	42/6

Prices include Envelopes to Match.

ONE OUT OF 100.

MORECAMBE BOY TO GO FOR LONDON AUDITION.

THIRTEEN-YEARS-OLD Eric Bartholomew, the well known local juvenile stage artiste, who has made such hits in local entertainments, has gone a step further in his career, for he has been chosen as one of the four finalists for the Lancashire and Cheshire area in the search-for-talent competition organised by the journal "Melody Maker."

The competition is linked up with Jack Hylton's radio and stage feature, "Youth Takes a Bow." The finalists in the area competition will travel to London for special auditions before Jack Hylton.

Young Bartholomew was one of ten competitors who succeeded in reaching the area final for Lancashire and Cheshire. There were one hunderd competitors in the area. The ten finalists appeared at the Kingsway Cinema, Hoylake, a week ago, when Eric was chosen with three others to travel to London. The other three were all girls from Liverpool.

"A BRILLIANT COMEDIAN ACT."

The "Melody Maker" report of the area final states:

"Eric Bartholomew put over a brilliant comedian act which caused the audience to roar with laughter.

'In an interview, he said 'My ambition is to become a comedian. My hero is George Formby, another native of Lancashire. I would certainly like to follow in his footsteps.'"

Eric won a talent-spotting competition at Morecambe Arcadian Theatre last month.

1940

"M.M." DISCOVERY ON STAGE WITH HYLTON

INCLUDED in the Jack Hylton radio feature "Youth Takes a Bow," presented on Monday of last week at the Nottingham Empire, with Brian Michie as compere, was a 13-years-old Morecambe boy Eric Bartholomew.

Eric was one of the many "Melody Maker" readers who were recently auditioned at Hoylake, under Mr. Jack Fallen's auspices.

He competed on the Friday night, and entered the final on the Saturday, when he was chosen as one of the four to appear before Jack Hylton himself.

I happened to be present myself (*writes Jerry Dawson*) when Jack Hylton auditioned these four acts in Manchester, and at the time he was very impressed by Eric's versatility.

In dance, in song, or in burlesque this youngster had all the aplomb of a seasoned performer, and obviously with the necessary experience, here was a winner.

So once again, the "Melody Maker" helps to set on the road to fame a youngster of whom more should be heard as he matures. He is entirely self-taught and before entering for the "Youth Takes a Bow" competition, won innumerable local contests and has appeared on the stage at the Winter Gardens, Morecambe.

Eric Bartholomew is the name—watch out for it!

...would be the first to acknowledge excellent playing support from Pamela Gibson as Portia, Robert Ginns as Antonio, and Lee Fox as Bassanio.

Merry Music Hall Bills

"Secrets of the B.B.C." at Birmingham Hippodrome is a merry collection of acts which stars Douglas Byng, Archie Glen and Dicky Hasset, with their respective and individual styles of humour. Others are Nick Cardello, an ace among card-sharpers; charming Celia Lipton, good as Deanna Durbin; Mariora, in deft juggling; the Redheads; and that genial giant Bryan Michie, with some of his youthful discoveries taking a bow, and Mary Naylor, a singer, and Eric Bartholomew, a comedian, taking the biggest. But for the older generation the best thing was Marie Lloyd, as recalled by her sisters, Alice and Rosie.

A speedy, colourful revue is at Aston Hippodrome this week. Produced by William Henshall and entitled "Une Nuit Excitante," it combines pace with spectacle, melody with humour.

The latter is provided in no small measure by Sid Field and noticeable in a good supporting

1940

THE SUNDAY TIMES

The Dramatic World

1940

ALL'S WELL WITH THE MUSIC HALL

By JAMES AGATE

Last week's performance at the New Theatre, Oxford, suggests that the British music hall, though possibly not *in situ* is still *in statu quo*. I pray that this is good Latin; now that the young men have gone down there is nobody in Oxford who understands the language. What I am trying to say is that our comics are in fine fettle and that, judging from last week, there is not likely to be a shortage of them.

But first let me deal with "The Dorchester Follies," a number of West End lovelies looking less like Pilgrims than coryphees from the Venusberg and waving walking-sticks which, for some explained reason, had come out all over apple-blossom. After this Mr. Maurice Winnick and his Orchestra, consisting, if my perceptions were in working order, of two trombones, two trumpets, four saxophones, piano, double-bass and drums, discoursed what the programme announced as "The Sweetest Music This Side of Heaven." Shade of Flaubert who, whenever he encountered monstrosity, would murmur, "*C'est gigantesque!*" Among the tunes was that arch-misnomer "Begin the Beguine," a misnomer since a béguine means a woman who shared the heresies of the béguards, these being a collection of thirteenth-century and somewhat obstreperous mendicants. The béguines were nuns from the Pays-Bas, who lived in convents without taking vows. "Fausse dévote" is the French phrase. Now you cannot begin a *dévote*, sham or otherwise. Why was not the profession content with the word without the "e," since a "béguin," as every Frenchman from Stendhal to Maurice Chevalier has known and preached, is "Une passion amoureuse et passagère"—surely I don't have to translate that?—or even "La personne qui en est l'objet." But ...

... motion to unheard of lengths. This performance had some of Irving's quality as Mephistopheles, the fascinating mixture of age-old diabolism and schoolboy cheek. And I must not forget Mr. Freddie Bamberger, a jesting pianist, who continually interrupted a study for the left hand, which I suspect to have been of his own composition, with shafts of wit which even the most enterprising among lance-corporals were sometimes slow to gather. And I suspect almost to certainty that the composer here was Mr. Bamberger himself.

The Contortionist

So much for the older half of the company. The younger announced itself under the heading "Youth takes a Bow." Or you might put it that Youth was on the prow and Mr. Brian Michie at the helm. There was a young lady who danced on long boots and was said to be the legitimate successor to Little Tich. But did this child *quite* remind us, as that great little artist reminded Jean Lorrain, of Constantin Guys, Daumier, Goya, Dickens and M. Prudhomme? Never mind, she did well enough. Then there was a small boy from Lancashire, spiritual descendant of Jack Pleasants, going about the world as a self-confessed loony and thereby enabled to pluck many kinds of fruit forbidden to the more amply witted. And then there was a mouth-organ expert with a command of tone and range which would have made the mouth of Berlioz water. I forget what it was that this prodigy played; I have no doubt that if a discharge of artillery had been required he would have simulated it.

I am not, as a rule, a lover of the contortionist's art. Whether or not it is Man's duty to remain in the station to which it has pleased Providence to call him, I have ...

ROUND THE THEATRES

1940

A Witty Revue

Stars And New Talent In Variety

By Our Dramatic Critic

"NINE SHARP." By Herbert Farjeon.—COURT.

This is *revue* in the original sense of the word, a satirical survey of contemporary fads and foibles. Mr. Farjeon ranges from casually ironic facetiousness to pungent, biting wit with unfailing resource; Walter Leigh's music is blithe and gay and matches the impish parody of the book in "Magyar Malady" and "'Voila les Non-Stop Nudes"; and Hedley Briggs's *décor* is cheerful and elegant.

At times the show is the victim of circumstances: some of Mr. Farjeon's ideas have been copied and the bloom is off their pristine freshness; we do not laugh as easily at eccentricities of the B.B.C.'s Empire enthusiasm as in more carefree days; and the full flavour of the Glyndebourne skit escapes those who have not seen the 5 o'clock trek in evening dress.

For the rest the show is great fun, and is put over with verve and precision by a cast prodigal in talent. Hermione Baddeley is diabolically clever in caricaturing her sex, all the way from the simpering girl to the croaking old lady of many operations, and her burlesque of an aged ballerina is just gorgeous. George Benson is always comically droll, and his Central European dancer, like an Epstein statue come to life, is brilliant parody. Many others give versatile support.—P.R.

EMPIRE.—Bulky Brian Michie has talented juveniles in "Youth Takes a Bow," and one expects success for Eric Bartholomew, who has a remarkable appreciation of the droll, and Dorothy Duval, a Liverpool girl with impersonations of Little Tich. Of other turns, Dicky Hassett provides fun in "large lumps," Adelaide Hall croons in her unique and delightful fashion. George Moon and Bertram Brown have new "gags," and Sam Rayne "a joke a second."

potential straight away, and so did the boys in the band. 'Bye, then, Ernie,' they teased him. 'Things won't be the same with this new lad around, but I dare say we'll soon get used to him. What are you going to do now?'[4] Hylton was complimentary but non-committal. 'Your boy has talent,' he told Sadie. 'Maybe we can use him.'[5] Eric returned home to Morecambe without exchanging a word with Ernie, but it wouldn't be long before their paths crossed again.

After several agonising months, Eric finally received the call that he (or rather Sadie) had been waiting for. Hylton wanted him to join the cast of Michie's new touring show, Youth Takes A Bow. Sadie had always been determined that her only son wouldn't end up 'tied to a whistle' like his father. This was only the beginning, but in a way, it was the biggest break he ever got. Eric made his professional debut at the Nottingham Empire, on a salary of £5 a week, plus expenses. Sadie went with him, as his chaperone.

Eric was lucky to have such supportive parents – a mother sufficiently committed and resourceful to accompany him on this Light Ent trek around the country, and a father sufficiently easy going to let her go. Such an arrangement would have been impossible if they'd had any other children. It was only because Eric was an only child that Sadie was able to spend so long away from home. When Ernie joined the cast in Swansea, he travelled there alone, as he had done ever since his first trip to London. His dad had long since returned to Leeds, to help Connie raise their other children. Harry Wiseman never found another partner to replace his son, but Ernie was more fortunate. Finally, at the Swansea Empire, the two halves of Britain's greatest double act were introduced to one another. Little did they know it, but their respective destinies were staring each other in the face.

Despite the affection that flowed between them during the forty five years that followed, Eric and Ernie's first encounter was hardly love at first sight. Ernie was already an established name. Eric was still a beginner. Ernie was on seven quid a week, compared with Eric's fiver. Far from greeting him as a kindred spirit, Eric thought Ernie was a bit of a bighead (although, as one of Britain's best known child stars, he actually had quite a lot to be bigheaded about). The first time Ernie caught Eric's act was when he saw him audition for Jack Hylton. The first time Eric caught Ernie's act was on the radio, performing with his hero, Arthur Askey. Ernie was fifteen and had already graduated to long trousers. Eric was still fourteen and still wore shorts that showed off his knobbly knees. Eric's jokes about Ernie's modest height and his short fat hairy legs had their origins in a time when Ernie towered over Eric, and the only short fat hairy legs on show were Eric's.

Although Eric and Ernie were now in the same show, they still carried on performing separately, and things probably would have stayed that way if it they hadn't ended up sharing the same room – and often the same bed. In those days, travelling entertainers were expected to sort out their own accommodation – and extraordinary as it may seem today, child entertainers were no different. Eric lodged with Sadie, but Ernie had to find his own digs. That he ended up with Eric and Sadie, rather than on his own, was largely the result of a little international dispute called World War Two.

At first, Adolf Hitler's impact on Youth Takes A Bow was confined to the odd air raid, but by the time the show reached Oxford in 1940, hostilities were in full swing. The town was full of troops, soldiers had snapped up virtually every bed, and Ernie found himself traipsing the darkened streets, without anywhere to spend the night. He called at every guest house he could find, until he arrived at the house were Eric and Sadie were lodging. The landlady told him they were fully booked, but Sadie took pity on him and invited him in to share Eric's bed. It was an arrangement they would repeat countless times on tour, and countless times on TV. From then on, Sadie took Ernie under her protective wing, treating him like an adoptive son.

Hitler also played his part in uniting Eric and Ernie as performers. When the boys reached Coventry, they found the city flattened by the Luftwaffe, and though the theatre was still standing, accommodation was so scarce throughout this devastated city that they had to lodge in Birmingham and travel into Coventry every day by train. Confined to a railway carriage for hours on end, their banter and tomfoolery became more and more frenetic, until a frazzled Sadie suggested they channel their energies into something more profitable than mere horseplay. 'Try and do a double act,' she told them. 'All you need are a few fresh jokes and a song.'[6] Eric and Ernie loved the idea, and although there was nothing fresh about the jokes they used (or reused, to be more accurate) right from the start, they enjoyed a special rapport, and a rare ability to make the stalest chestnuts crackle. They still did their solo spots every night, but they practised their double act every day – even buying a tape recorder, so they could polish their joint routines.

In 1941, Eric and Ernie finally persuaded Hylton to let them try out together in front of a paying public. They made their debut as a double act at the Liverpool Empire, and when the company travelled on to Scotland, Hylton was sufficiently impressed to retain this new turn in the show. There was only one problem. Michie thought Bartholomew & Wise was too much of a mouthful. Hylton had already persuaded Ernie to change his surname. Now it was Eric's turn to find another name. Michie

Eric with harmonica player Arthur Tolcher. Years later, Tolcher would become one of Eric and Ernie's most celebrated sidekicks, as 'Not Now Arthur' in the Morecambe & Wise Show.

suggested Barlow or Bartlett (the maiden name, as it turned out, of Eric's future wife) but Eric didn't like the sound of either. Thankfully, one of the show's adult entertainers came to the rescue, an American called Bert Hicks. Hicks recalled a showbiz friend back home who'd used his home town as a stage name, and so Bartholomew & Wiseman were reborn as Morecambe & Wise.

Left: **Eric stepping out with mystery companion. Where is she now?**

Below: **Eric's first music hall routine.**

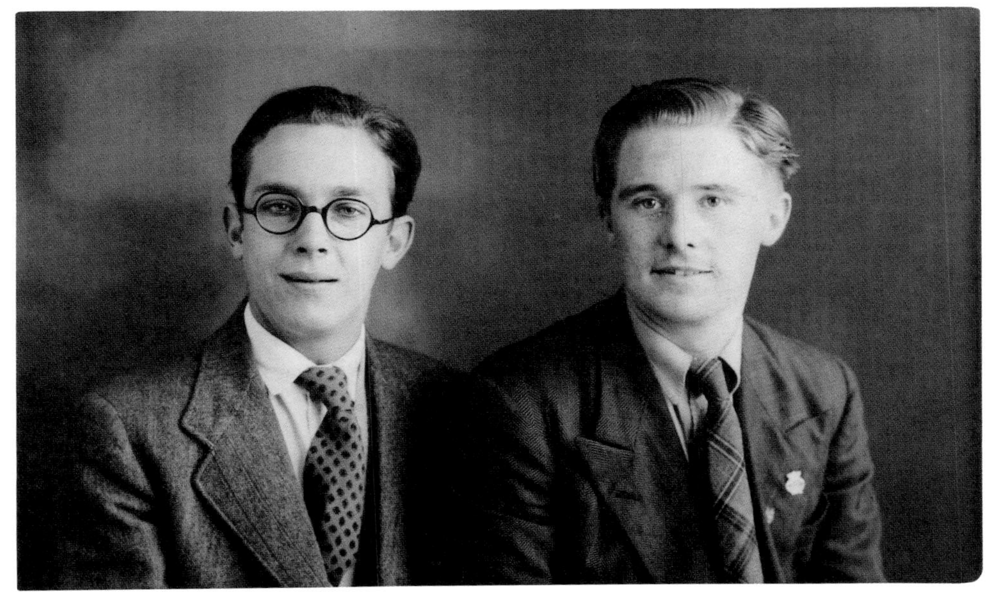

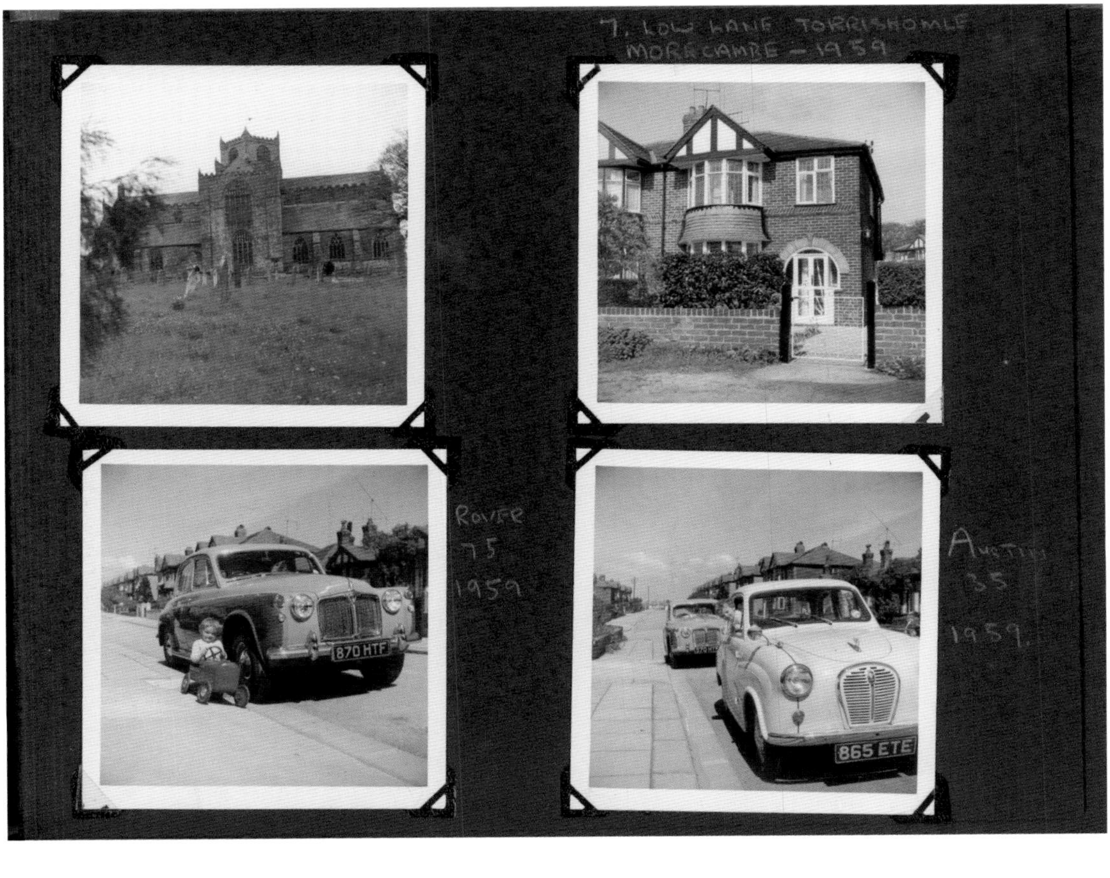
7, LOW LANE TORRISHOLME
MORECAMBE – 1959
Rover 75 1959
870 HTF
Austin 35 1959
865 ETE

BRISTOL

MOLLY
ST LEONARDS 50
SYLVIA ENGLAND
SYLVIA 50

CANDIE GARDENS
Nightly at 8'is.
VARIETY
MORECAMBE AND WISE
BOB NELSON
GABRIELLE
THE ROYALETTES
MARY PRIESTMAN
NOW OPEN
The GUERNSEY PRESS
BOOK HERE
After the Show
ICES
Open Dai
SUNDAY

ME.

Chapter 4

Morecambe & Wise

Ernie: You're making us look like a cheap music hall act.

Eric: Well, we are a cheap music hall act.

In normal circumstances, Eric and Ernie's successful debut might have been enough to set them up as a promising new double act, but the war that had brought them together now pulled them apart. By 1942, the travails of staging a touring show in wartime finally proved impossible, and less than a year after their first turn together,

Youth Takes A Bow took its final bow. Eric and Ernie were both keen to carry on, but they were still only sixteen, and even without a war on, the transition from child stars to grown up pros was always going to be tough. Such an arduous proposition was too much even for the ever resourceful Sadie. She returned to Morecambe, and her eternally patient husband. Eric went with her. He clocked on at the local razor blade factory, where he proved to be every bit as useless as he had been back at school. His weekly wage was just seventeen and six – barely more than he used to earn for a couple of spots at a local working men's club when he was a kid. For a lad who'd been on a fiver a week, it was a pretty steep comedown, but he wouldn't have been the first child star (or the last) who failed to make the grade. As he toiled ten hours a day, for a few pennies an hour, Eric could have been forgiven for thinking that was that.

Ernie, meanwhile, had travelled down to London, where he found the sort of digs aspiring showmen usually only find in Hollywood movies – lodging with a family of Japanese acrobats. However he had less luck finding work. The Blitz had taken its toll on London's variety theatres, and having obtained no bookings whatsoever, he was forced to return home to Yorkshire, where the only opening he could find was a supporting role on the local coal round. After three months, he could bear no more. Desperate for a change of scene, and a change of occupation, he went to stay with Eric, to try and get some gigs together in Morecambe. With no local bookings to speak of, Sadie finally relented and accompanied Eric and Ernie to London. There, in 1943, thanks to her tireless hustling, they secured a position in a show called Strike A New Note at ten quid each a week. They probably could have held out for more, but it was still a lot better than delivering coal or making razor blades. Yet there was one creative hitch. The producer, George Black, didn't want them to do a double act. In that case, said Ernie, they weren't interested. In that case, replied Black, they could understudy his second string comic, Alec Pleon. Eric and Ernie could still be bossed around when it came to money, but when it came to the act itself, they already had exceptional self belief.

As it happened, Ernie's negotiating triumph was a pretty hollow victory. Pleon, recollected Ernie ruefully, turned out to be the fittest man in show business, and Eric and Ernie were reduced to the role of 'glorified chorus boys.'[1] Yet a walk on part in a successful show is a lot better than a leading role in a flop, and Strike A New Note was such a big hit that even these chorus boys could bask in its reflected glory. The star of the show was Sid Field, a superb Brummie comic who was still relatively unknown down south. Strike A New Note made Field's name in London. Visiting Americans like Clark Gable and James Stewart came along to see him, and even dropped in backstage. Eric and Ernie were still a long way from Hollywood, but now a little bit of Hollywood had come to them. The experience did wonders for their self esteem, whetting their appetite for stardom and bolstered their belief that they might really make it after all. The BBC broadcast a version of the show, followed by a series, Youth Must Have Its Swing. After a couple of false starts, it seemed Eric and Ernie were on their way.

Yet just as they were getting going again, Hitler intervened once more. Ernie was called up, and chose to enlist in the Merchant Navy. It was either that or the Army, or

ERIC
ERNIE
MORECAMBE and WISE

going down the mines. Ernie had hoped to see the world. Instead he was lumbered with the mundane task of ferrying coal from Newcastle to Battersea Power Station. As Eric said, 'the nearest he got to action was seeing a knife fight in Gateshead.'[2] However anything more glamorous would have taken him overseas for months at a time, and might quite conceivably have got him killed. Instead, during his frequent spells of shore leave between these dreary but relatively brief voyages, Ernie was able to keep his hand in as a solo entertainer in the halls. Fate, in its roundabout way, had smiled on Eric and Ernie, but it would still be a while before they worked together again.

Since Eric was six months younger than Ernie, it was another six months before he was called up. He stayed on in Strike A New Note until it closed, then joined ENSA, the Entertainments National Service Association (or Every Night Something Awful, as it was affectionately known) but in the summer of 1944, he turned eighteen, and was sent down the mines as a 'Bevin Boy'.[3] As an alternative to armed conscription, the chances of being shot at were pretty slim, but that was just about all it had going for it. For a fit young man, it would have been purgatory. For Eric, it was hell.

Eric in panto.

One of the few perks of this dismal job was that you could choose which mine you went down. Eric's dad suggested Accrington, since they had relations there who could put him up. His Accrington relatives looked after him well enough, packing him off to work at half past five each morning with a cooked breakfast inside him, but as for the mine itself, he could scarcely have made a worse choice. This pit had been condemned twenty years before, and some of the seams were only two feet high. After less than a year, Eric was invalided out with heart trouble. It was a sinister foretaste of things to come.

Unfortunately, Eric was still well enough to return to the razor blade factory – but fortunately, Sadie came to the rescue once again. She'd heard about a travelling show called Lord John Sanger's Circus & Variety. 'Lord' John's brother, Edward Sanger, had worked on Youth Takes A Bow, and knew Eric already. Sadie encouraged Eric to get in touch. 'As it happens,' Edward told him, 'we have just engaged a comic, but you can be his feed.'[4] That comic, on £12 a week to Eric's £10, was none other than Ernie Wise.

'Even as the straight man, Eric got the big laughs,'[5] said Ernie, and that wasn't the only thing wrong with this sorry mongrel of a show. Like most showbiz flops, the actual concept was a good one – to take Variety entertainers to towns too small to have their own theatres, and combine these turns with circus acts, all under the same big top. In reality, it was the worst of both worlds – neither circus nor Variety, but something half-baked inbetween. Lord Sanger was no more aristocratic than Duke Ellington or Count Basie, and the ersatz nature of this enterprise was epitomised by his pet shop menagerie – no big cats, merely some performing dogs and pigeons, a couple of hamsters, a llama, a wallaby, a parrot and a donkey.

Unluckily for Eric and Ernie, one of the few ways in which Sanger's show did resemble a proper circus was that everyone (apart from Sanger) was expected to muck in. The performers had to put up the big top, set out the seats and even sell the tickets – not that they sold that many. The big top held seven hundred, but on at least one occasion they ended up playing to single figures, and it came as no surprise when their

Eric and friend.

pay was virtually cut in half. Ernie's wages were reduced to £7, and Eric's to £5 – exactly what they'd been earning in Youth Takes A Bow eight years before.

Offstage, if anything, things were even worse. Eric and Ernie were obliged to sleep in an old RAF trailer, wash in a canvas bucket, eat their meals around a camp fire and shit in a hole in the ground. For a pair who'd tasted the high life in two hit shows, it was yet another bitter comedown. Ernie, at least, met his future wife Doreen in the show, but for Eric there were no such romantic compensations. When Sanger finally called a halt, in 1947, Britain's greatest double act went their separate ways once more.

They might have never met again if it hadn't been for one of those improbable coincidences which seem completely implausible in fiction, but are actually a frequent feature of real life. Sadie and Eric had returned to London, to try and find an agent, and were walking down Regent Street when they bumped into Ernie. Ernie was also looking for work, and living in digs in Brixton. Sadie invited him to share their lodgings in Chiswick. 'You too might as well be out of work together as separately,'[6] she said. Throughout the forty odd years that followed, they would never work apart again.[7]

Today Chiswick is a bustling suburb, full of fashionable cafes and restaurants, where even the smallest terraced houses sell for half a million quid. However when Eric and Ernie lived here, it was a sleepy, rather scruffy place, on the very edge of London, an awfully long way from the bright lights of the West End and the smart theatres of Shaftesbury Avenue – what Eric regarded as the centre of the world. Not that they had much cause to go Up West, since their entire act still only stretched to ten minutes. 'If

Right to Left: Ernie, his fiancée Doreen, Eric and Mystery Companion.

Eric puts a brave face on life under canvas, washing his own smalls while touring with Lord Sanger's Variety circus.

Not much of a dressing room, but the best that Lord Sanger could provide.

the manager wanted twelve minutes then we did the same act only slower,' said Ernie. 'If we didn't get any laughs, we could do it in six.'[8] And during the fourteen months they spent here, they only got six weeks work. Sadie went back out to work as a char lady, but Eric and Ernie didn't even think about getting day jobs. 'We were variety artists,' said Ernie. 'We were pros. To consider anything else would have been heresy.'[9] This uncompromising attitude sounds pretty arrogant in retrospect, especially when Sadie was out on her hands and knees, scrubbing other people's floors. However you need a bit of arrogance to make it in show business, and Sadie knew better than anyone that a day job could easily become a job for life. Like many bright mothers who've been denied the chance to better themselves, she set about bettering her children. And to her eternal credit, she always treated Ernie like a second child.

Yet even with Sadie's charring, and Ernie's rapidly dwindling bank book, they often couldn't pay their rent for months on end. That they weren't flung out onto the street, and forced to find more gainful employment, was entirely due to their benevolent landlady, Mrs Eleanor Duer. Her boarding house, at 13 Clifton Gardens, may not have looked like much from the outside, but she had an illustrious history of accommodating theatricals, and she was uncommonly sympathetic when these fledgling comics pleaded for a bit more time to pay. Among her many showbiz guests were Wilson, Kepple & Betty, who did a wonderfully silly Egyptian sand dance that was a legend in the old music halls. Years later, Eric and Ernie would perform a spoof tribute of this classic act on television. In a way, it was also a tribute to Nell Duer.

They finally got their big break through Vivian Van Damm's (in)famous Windmill Theatre, though truth be told, Van Damm (aka VD) could hardly have done less to help. The forerunner of Soho strip clubs like Paul Raymond's Revuebar, the Windmill was permitted to show women in various states of undress, so long as they didn't move. The result was a series of surreal (and often downright silly) nude tableaux, in a variety of implausible (and implausibly flimsy) costumes. To fill the gaps between scene changes, punters were treated to a succession of front of curtain turns by a series of (fully clothed) comedians. All in all, it was a typically British blue revue – coy, furtive, and promising far more than it delivered.

Today the Windmill is renowned as the birthplace of a generation of great comics, but VD actually turned down almost as many future stars as he hired. True, he booked Dick Emery, Jimmy Edwards and Nicholas Parsons, but he rejected Roy Castle, Norman Wisdom and Benny Hill. And even though he hired three of the Goons (Michael Bentine, Harry Secombe and Peter Sellers) he turned down the funniest Goon of all, Spike Milligan. 'Van Damm was not one of the world's great judges of comedy,' reflects Parsons. 'It is ironic to think that such a man should have been running a theatre whose reputation is now based on all the famous comedians who worked there.'[10] Well, the Windmill may be famous for its comedians now, but that certainly wasn't what made it famous at the time. Apart from their purely practical role, as a sort of walking talking intermission, Windmill comics performed much the same function as the articles in top shelf magazines.

Eric and Ernie never were a top shelf act, and they felt ill at ease in these salacious surroundings. Theirs was always a family show, and although the Windmill was terribly tame by modern standards, without a family audience they were lost. They were booked to play six shows a day for one week – and if things worked out, five weeks to

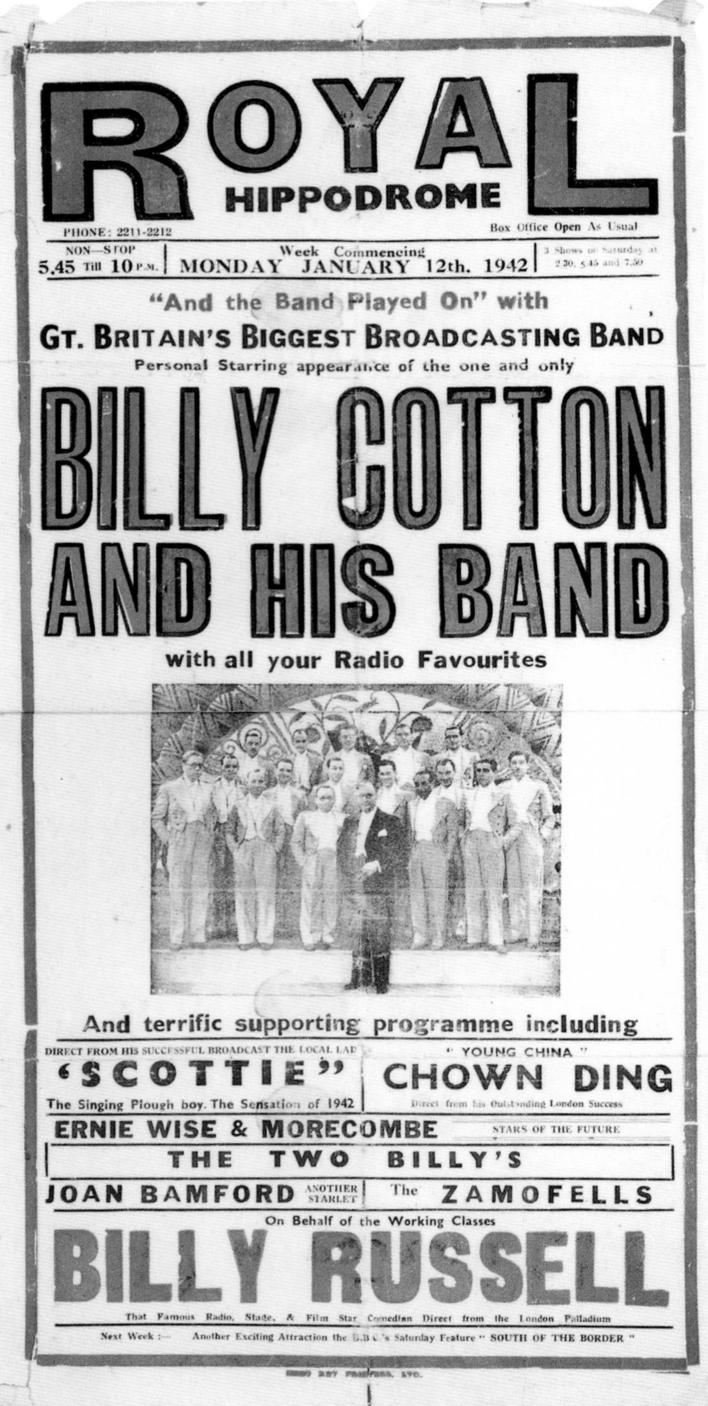

Left: **At this early stage in their career, Ernie was still a bigger draw than Eric (they couldn't even spell his name right) as their uneven billing on this poster shows. Bandleader Billy Cotton was the father of Bill Cotton Junior, the TV executive who later gave Eric & Ernie their own BBC show.**

Right: **Proper billing by now (and proper spelling too). Frank Pope was Eric & Ernie's first proper agent, and the promoter who really cemented their reputation in the halls. Pope became a close friend, and was even godfather to Eric's son, Gary. Yet unlike a lot of other Variety acts, Eric and Ernie quickly recognised the vast potential of television, and when they saw that live Variety was dying, they decided, with regret, that they had no choice but to leave Pope for another agent who could get them TV work, the legendary Billy Marsh.**

THE PREMIER VARIETY JOURNAL

THE PERFORMER

THE OFFICIAL ORGAN OF THE VARIETY ARTISTES' FEDERATION

Vol. XCV No. 2428 THURSDAY, DECEMBER 4, 1952. [Registered at the G.P.O. as a Newspaper] Price 6d.

MR. J.E. BARTHOLOMEW

BRITISH PASSPORT

UNITED KINGDOM OF GREAT BRITAIN AND NORTHERN IRELAND

1779812

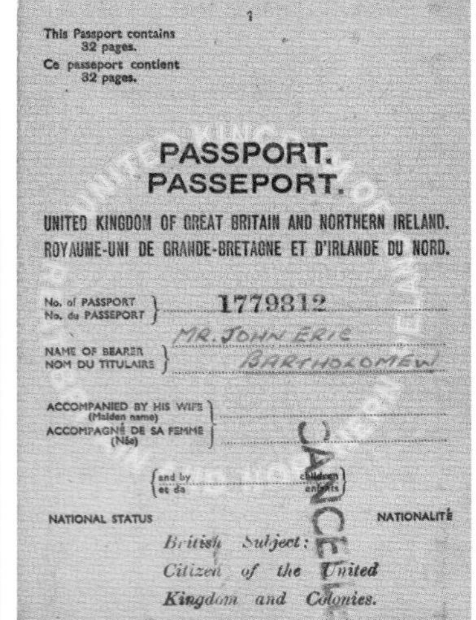
1

This Passport contains 32 pages.
Ce passeport contient 32 pages.

PASSPORT.
PASSEPORT.

UNITED KINGDOM OF GREAT BRITAIN AND NORTHERN IRELAND.
ROYAUME-UNI DE GRANDE-BRETAGNE ET D'IRLANDE DU NORD.

No. of PASSPORT / No. du PASSEPORT: 1779812

NAME OF BEARER / NOM DU TITULAIRE: MR. JOHN ERIC BARTHOLOMEW

ACCOMPANIED BY HIS WIFE (Maiden name) / ACCOMPAGNÉ DE SA FEMME (Née)

(and by / et de) children / enfants

NATIONAL STATUS / NATIONALITÉ

British Subject: Citizen of the United Kingdom and Colonies.

CANCELLED

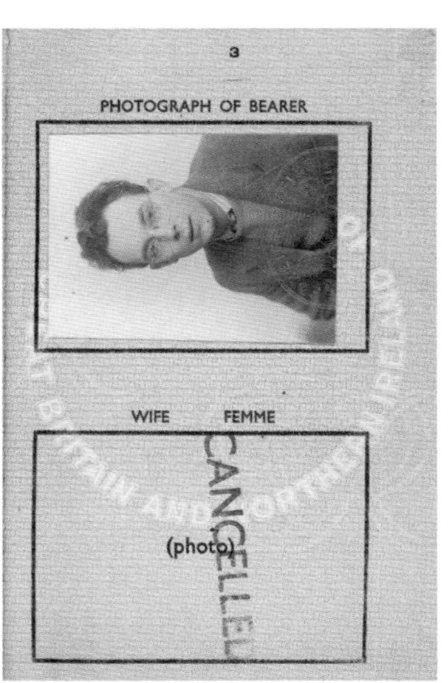
3

PHOTOGRAPH OF BEARER

WIFE FEMME

(photo)

CANCELLED

R.B.1
15

MINISTRY OF FOOD

SERIAL NO. BE 603007

1952-1953

RATION BOOK

(GENERAL)

Surname BARTHOLOMEW Initials J.E.

Address 43 Christie Ave

Morecambe

IF FOUND RETURN TO ANY FOOD OFFICE		FOOD OFFICE CODE No. EW 1

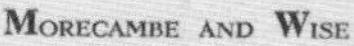
MORECAMBE AND WISE

Georg Bartram.	£461-16-6d.
Photographs.	£7-13-6d.
Stage Suits	£154-16-6d.
Script	£31-10-0
Charity	£16-5-6
Adverts	£35-11-0
Music	£4-0-0
V.A.F.	£9-18-0

These are the figures we have actually spent. We have to agree on the expenses.

Eric.

Right: **Eric took this photo of his friend and colleague, Harry Secombe.**

follow. After dying six times a day for the first three days, VD told them he was letting them go, in favour of another double act called Hank & Scott. Most young comics would have slunk off with their tails between their legs, but Eric and Ernie had the humility and foresight to ask Van Damm a favour. Would he please put an advert in The Stage, announcing they were leaving the Windmill due to prior commitments, and of their own accord? VD agreed, and Eric and Ernie went away and wrote to twenty agents, inviting them to see the show.

No one came to see them the next day, and no one turned up the day after, but on their last day at the Windmill, one of the agents they'd written to finally arrived. They had to buy him a ticket (VD wouldn't give them a comp) but it was a good investment. This agent got them a spot in another nude show called Fig Leaves & Apple Sauce at the Clapham Grand in South London, and though they stiffed in the first half with their established set, they went back on in the second half with some hastily written new material and brought the house down. Offers flooded in and before the year was out they found their first regular agent, Frank Pope, who booked the all important Moss Empire circuit, with two dozen big venues around the country and the London Palladium at its peak. After more than a decade in the business, Morecambe & Wise were a proper variety act at last.

In the end, it had been a close run thing, and the show that put them on the right track had very nearly finished them. Years later, Eric and Ernie were still sufficiently mindful of this narrow escape to refuse Van Damm's request to put their names on his self aggrandising roll of honour. Yet at least they could console themselves that they hadn't been fired to make way for a couple of no hopers. The double act that Van Damm preferred, Hank & Scott, consisted of a pianist called Derek Scott and a comedian called Tony Hancock. Maybe VD wasn't quite so bad at spotting comic talent after all.

ERNIE TED.SHINE
BRIGHTON 51.
SELF - ALLAN
BRIGHTON
1951
ALLAN CLIVE
BRIGHTON. 51

ALLAN - ERNIE - TED.
BRIGHTON
KATHIE
TERRY
ERNIE
SELF.
BARNET
51

LETA. PARIS. 51.
LETA APRIL
PARIS
51
SELF. APRIL
1951 PARIS.

SELF WANDA
U.M.
LOMMOND
51
SHIRL. SELF. WANDA
LOMOND
SCOT
51.
WANDA
U.S.M.
LOMOND
51

DOREEN SELF
DOREENS 21ST
SELF 25TH BIRTHDAY
1951
YES
DOREEN
51

DOREEN
51
SELF D. F
51
S. D. E
51

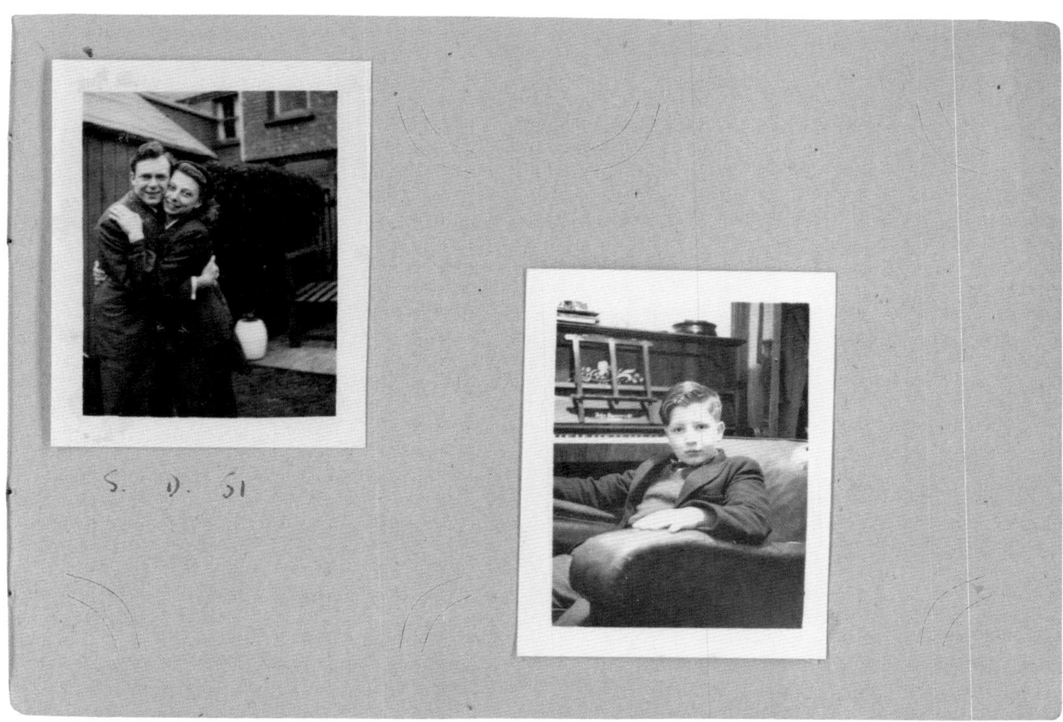
S. D. 51

JACKIE
JUDY ERNIE
THE DOG
MARY ERNIE MARG.
MARY

Eric Morecambe
Snapshots

Audrey
Ernie
Doris
Audrey
Myself
Doris
Myself
Myself
Audrey
and
Myself
Audrey

Chapter 5

THE VARIETY YEARS

Ernie: What shall we do today?

Eric: Let's toss a coin. Heads we'll go to the dog racing. Tails we'll go to the football. If it comes down on its edge, we'll go to work.

MORECAMBE & WISE

THAT WAS ERIC and Ernie's first proper joke, but like most of their early jokes, it wasn't theirs. They'd nicked it from another double act – Ernie's old double act, Carson & Kid. And they didn't just plunder jokes from Ernie's dad. Any other comic was fair game. Nowadays, there's practically nothing worse than accusing a comedian of stealing someone else's material, but back then pinching gags was common practice. Jokers

Joan Bartlett, the future Mrs Eric Morecambe, Miss Margate 1951.

Eric and Joan's wedding day, 1952. Ernie looks a bit left out, but he needn't have worried. He was married himself six months later.

Eric's wife Joan in her modeling days. Understandably, her gentleman admirer seems in no hurry to finish his pint.

Eric and Joan's wedding, 1952.

Eric and Joan cut the cake. The couple on the right are Eric's mum and dad, George and Sadie.

The show was a smash hit but there was nothing remotely glamorous about Joan and Eric's new life together on the road. Their digs were bleak, and the weather was awful. There was thick snow on the ground, and the smoke from the factory chimneys turned the fog to filthy smog. 'It was a dreadful winter, bitterly cold,' recalls Joan, with a shudder. 'What a way to start your married life.'

Galvanised by Eric's rapid nuptials, Ernie and Doreen tied the knot in January 1953, after an epic five year courtship. Eric was best man, but by now Joan was already pregnant. They never planned to have a child so soon. 'It must have been the cold digs,'[4] said Eric, but Sheffield played hell with her pregnancy. In the end, she became so poorly that Eric had to pack her off to Morecambe for some fresh sea air. 'A few days in Morecambe, and I was as right as ninepence,' she says. 'As soon as I got back to Sheffield, I would be violently sick. Not a very romantic start to your life together.'

In September 1953, nine months after their wedding, Joan gave birth to a girl called Gail, in George and Sadie's house in Morecambe (Eric and Ernie were onstage at Blackpool's Winter Gardens at the time). Eric and Joan were both delighted with their new addition, but they'd had no time for courting. Aptly, Eric's favourite definition of a baby was 'last year's pleasure with lungs.' After the Sheffield run finished, Eric and Ernie went on tour, and for a while, Joan and Gail went with them. Yet the best they could afford was a succession of boarding houses with shared facilities – fine for a single man, but pretty miserable for a pair of newly weds with a newborn child. 'Touring with Gail was a nightmare,' says Joan. 'You didn't even have your own sitting room.' The three of them all had to sleep in the same bedroom, which didn't do much for Eric's rest and recuperation between shows. 'Anyone who sleeps like a baby doesn't have one,' he said, sardonically. Even the travelling was a trial. Eric didn't drive, so they did it all by train, cross country every Sunday, often with several changes along the way. Eventually they bought a house in Finchley, which was much better for Joan and Gail, although it meant they saw a lot less of Eric, since he was often away on tour.

A few months after Gail was born, Eric and Ernie landed their own TV series. Actually, it was a wonder nobody had thought of approaching them before. Their material may have been second hand, but their delivery was remarkably modern, and their conversational style was perfect for television. As Michael Grade told their biographer, Graham McCann, they were the first double act to really talk (and really listen) to each other, rather than firing all their gags straight at the audience. This naturalistic attitude was just what television needed. Unfortunately, in 1954 television had other plans.

Above: **A season in pantomime was a crucial part of any entertainer's annual income, and Eric & Ernie were happy to return to Sheffield for the second year running, even though Joan had spent a horrid few months here the year before. Stan Stennett often appeared with Eric & Ernie in panto, and compered Eric's last ever performance, thirty years later, on the very evening that he died.**

AN
ABC THEATRE
PROGRAMME
1/-
THE
MORECAMBE
& WISE
SHOW

Eric and Ernie pitched their own ideas to their producer, but the BBC brought in half a dozen of their own writers, and like newcomers in any new place of work, Eric and Ernie did what they were told. 'We'll do exactly as they say because these are the experts and we don't know anything about television,' they decided. It was a mistake they'd never make again, but it was a painful lesson nonetheless. The show was called Running Wild, and the reviews were savage. 'Definition of the week,' wrote Kenneth Bailey in The People. 'TV set: the box in which they buried Morecambe & Wise.'[5]

In retrospect, this critical mauling seems rather perplexing – especially since Eric and Ernie were hardly household names. Running Wild was certainly no masterpiece, but it wasn't really any worse than an awful lot of other stuff on telly at that time. Yet although Eric and Ernie were already old hands in the variety halls, on TV they were still beginners – and as outsiders in this strange new world, they simply didn't have the self confidence to laugh off this lurid assault on their reputations. 'You can't really explain television fear,' reflected Eric, years later. 'It's the type of fear, I should imagine, that an oyster gets at low tide.' Eric and Ernie were so rattled, they went to see the BBC's Head of Light Entertainment, Ronnie Waldman (the man who'd hired them in the first place) and begged him to take them off the air. 'We're scared to death,' said Ernie. 'We'd like to pull out.' 'Not on your life,' replied Waldman. 'Stick it out. I have faith in you.'[6] Reluctantly, Eric and Ernie saw out the remainder of their contract, and the show limped along to the end of its allotted six week run. Waldman's faith was

Eric (left), Ernie (right) and Harry Secombe (centre) in panto.

justified, though not by Running Wild. There was no magic turnaround, yet his wise counsel kept the studio door ajar for the TV comeback that would eventually arrive. The stress brought Ernie out in boils, but Eric's skin was thicker. 'Critics should be beaten to a pulp,' he said, 'and converted back into paper.' For the rest of his life, he carried a copy of Bailey's putdown in his wallet. It showed how much the review had stung, but it also showed his determination to refute it.

In the short term, however, there were no other TV offers forthcoming, so Eric and Ernie went back to the work they knew best. Live Variety was a world they understood, where they could stand or fall on their own merits, without a bunch of busybodies telling them what to do. 'I was on TV last week,' ran one of their gags mocking the medium that had spurned them. 'They said money was no object, so they didn't give me any.' 'I watched TV last night for three hours,' ran another. 'Then I discovered I was sat in front of a washing machine.' However their televisual trauma had taught them an important lesson. Running Wild had stifled the interplay between them, the interplay upon which all double acts depend. Henceforth, they would focus

Eric turns out for the Showbiz XI, in one of their regular charity matches at Blackpool FC's famous Bloomfield Road ground. Among their star players were comedians Stan Stennett (standing, third left), Tommy Cooper (standing, third right), Eric (kneeling, front left), Ernie (standing, second left) and Britain's greatest ever footballer, Sir Stanley Matthews (kneeling, centre).

on their relationship, to the exclusion of all else. The jokes were still important, but from now on they were never more than a means to an end.

They wrote themselves a new act, tailored to the particular dynamics of their partnership, and began their live comeback in the humdrum environs of Manchester's Ardwick Hippodrome. They were only fourth on the bill (so much for the omnipotent power of television) but they got a standing ovation. From then on, as a live act, they never looked back. As their confidence grew, they stopped lifting material from other acts and started creating unique routines that projected their own personalities. 'We used to do a routine with crisps,' recalled Eric. 'The stage staff hated us for it. I would eat them from a bag while Ernie was singing. He'd put his hand out and I'd put a crisp in his hand. Of course by the end of the week there was a great big grease mark on the stage which they could never get out. Usually we were followed by an animal act – dogs or seals or bears.'[7]

The stage staff may have hated this routine, but the animals enjoyed the leftovers. Yet it wasn't all fun and games. Many of the bigger theatres had seen better days, and some of the smaller venues were downright tawdry. The ambience in these spit and sawdust clubs is encapsulated in Mr Lonely, the sinister showbiz novel which Eric wrote in 1981:

'Dancing was thrown in, rowdies were thrown out, and, now and again, dinner was thrown up. Gambling, if permitted, was always kept well away from the entertainment because the management did not like the audience to hear the cheers of a man who had just won seventy quid, or the screams of a man who had just lost seven hundred quid, although they were less against the cheers than the screams. If the star name was big, so was the business; if the star name was not big, neither was the business. Service was normally slow, but what's the rush anyway. The waiters were mainly foreign, the waitresses were usually British, and the customer was often hungry. Invariably the room was dark; only the staff could see their way around because God has given all nightclub waiters special eyes. The toilets were sometimes as far away, or so it felt, as the next town.'[8]

As Eric used to say, 'Cleanliness is next to godliness, but in a Sheffield night club it's next to impossible.' 'I'm not really sweating – I'm just defrosting,' he'd say, when things got really sticky. In these fleapits, they had to find a gag for every eventuality, in order to survive. To an unresponsive punter: 'What do you do for a living? You are living, aren't you?' To an impertinent musician: 'When did you learn to play? I know it was today but what time today?' To a band leader who didn't know his place: 'I'll show you up for the fake you are. Play a baton solo.' And if another act outstayed their welcome: 'I thought chewing gum was hard to get off the stage.'

If all else failed, they could always find an emaciated punter to pick on. 'Were there any other survivors? There's going to be trouble when they open the coffin and find him gone.' They were never nasty, but they toughened up, and in time they became masters at warming up even the coldest room: 'That's what I like about this audience. They're going for silent laughter. You see that bloke with his eyes closed? He's not asleep. He's in hysterics.'

By 1956, they were back on the box, in a string of guest appearances, one of which was almost scuppered by the arrival of Eric's son, Gary. On the day of this recording, Joan had gone into labour, and Eric was a nervous wreck. 'I've got to know she's alright before I can work,' he said. Right on cue, Joan gave birth, Eric dashed to hospital see the baby and then dashed back to London to do the show. Thanks to Joan's prompt delivery, he was just in time for both appointments. It was typical of his frenetic schedule.

However it was their tour of Australia, which (in a roundabout way) really brought Eric and Ernie back to TV. Their trip Down Under went very well (Joan and Doreen came too – Gail and Gary went to stay with George and Sadie in Morecambe) but following a three month run in Melbourne, and another three months in Sydney, they came back to Blighty with a bump. TV had been gnawing away at Variety's audience for several years, but after six months away they really noticed the difference. A lot of theatres had closed, a lot more looked set to follow, and though they were booked to play a full summer season in Blackpool (at a princely 250 quid a week) they had nothing lined up thereafter. Variety would stagger on for a good while yet, but Eric and Ernie could see that its glory days were long gone.

It's a rotten job, but somebody's got to do it.

Most Variety acts kept on plodding along, hoping that something would turn up. Eric and Ernie were more decisive. They decided their

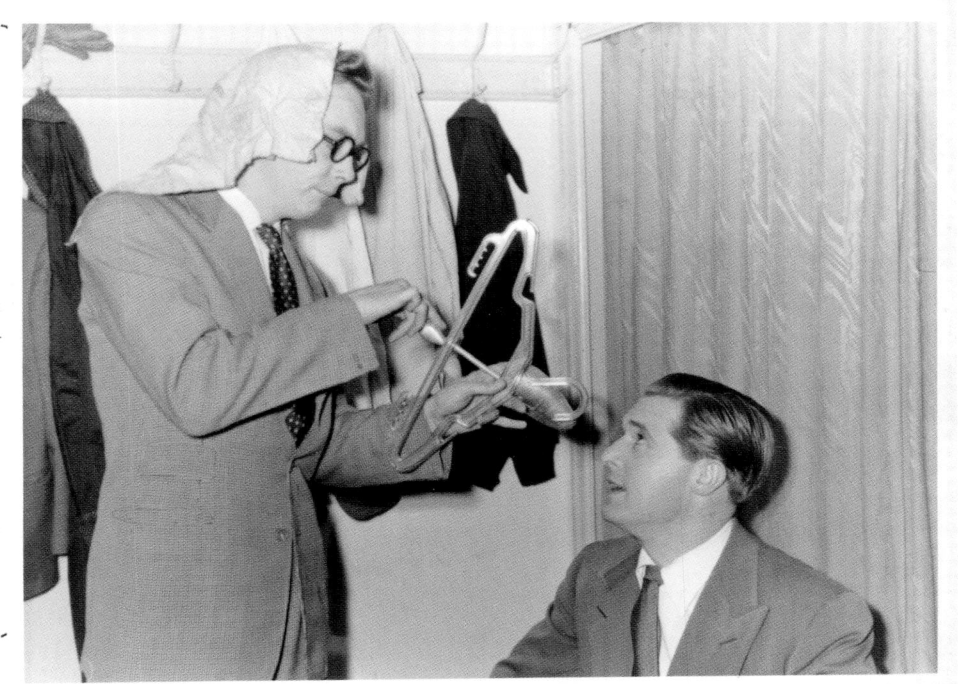

Above: **Eric and Ernie in Blackpool, doing their bit for women's lib.** Below: **Eric and Ernie in panto.**

NATIONAL CYCLING PROFICIENCY

SCHIMMELPENNINCK

Happy campers. Left to right: Doreen, Gail, Ernie, Gary, Eric, Joan. Summer Season, Weymouth, 1960.

future lay in TV after all, and for that they needed a new agent. They left their old agent, Frank Pope, whose main contacts were in Variety, and teamed up with Billy Marsh, whose TV contacts were unrivalled. 'Television gobbles up material,' Marsh warned them at the outset, 'but if you can keep coming up with good, fresh stuff, I can get you all the TV you want.'[9] Marsh was as good as his word. Guest spots flooded in, including a dozen appearances on Sunday Night At The London Palladium. Finally, in 1961, ATV offered them their own series. Seven years after their BBC debacle, TV had given them a second chance. And this time, they were determined to take it.

CONCERT

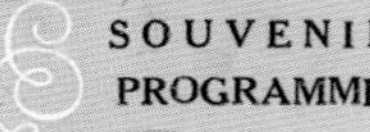

MORECAMBE and WISE

Introductions are really superfluous to such a star-spangled team of stage, radio and TV celebrities as appears in to-night's stage version of " Variety Fanfare."

You have heard all of them on the air frequently, not only in " Fanfare "—radio's slickest and fastest-moving variety series—but also in many other top-line shows.

Emerging as a star in his own right KEN FRITH with his "Magic Pianos" act after so long as the anonymous pianist of the BBC Northern Variety Orchestra.

You may remember his deft wizardry on the keys in the Ken Frith Trio that was such a popular spot in the Dave Morris "Club Night" series.

MORECAMBE AND WISE first broadcast in "Fanfare" six months ago and have deservedly earned their place as resident comedians in the series.

54 THE PERFORMER CHRISTMAS NUMBER, 1952

MORECAMBE & WISE

Extend the Season's Greetings to All Friends

Pantomime:
"Dick Whittington"
LYCEUM THEATRE, SHEFFIELD

Direction - - **FRANK POPE, 35, PANTON STREET, HAYMARKET, S.W.1**

Radio Fun.

★ MORECAMBE AND WISE ★

Popular New-Style Radio and Stage Comedians Talk to YOU.

HULLO, RADIO FUN pals!

This is Eric Morecambe calling you—and I'm doing the talking for my partner, Ernie Wise, too.

How did we gain success on the radio and reach the dizzy heights of the London Palladium? Well, it all started at school.

Both Ernie and I played in school concerts, although we had no ideas at that time about going on the stage.

Later, we were asked to appear in charity shows, too, and people seemed to like our act, so we decided to wait our chance and enter a talent contest as soon as one came our way.

It was at one of these talent competitions that the producer, Brian Michie, saw us, and he invited us to join his show "Youth Takes a Bow."

We were with this show for three years, but ou road to success began with broadcasting in "Variety Fanfare." We wrote comedy scripts about famous characters in history. People wrote in to the B.B.C. and asked to hear more—and that was the beginning.

Our favourite part—the one which we and the audience seem to get most fun from—is playing "Captain and Mate" in the pantomime "Dick Whittington."

Needless to say, we enjoy our job of making people laugh and would not change to any other, although a stage career is harder work than most people imagine. The only recipe for success is rehearse, rehearse, and KEEP ORIGINAL.

During the war I was what was known as a "Bevin Boy" and worked in the coal mines, while Ernie Wise went into the Merchant Navy.

Our most exciting experience happened when we were on tour with a circus. We were riding in a five-ton lorry, going down a steep hill, when the brakes failed!

Halfway down the hill were traffic lights—and they were at red! All the time the lorry was gathering speed. Can you imagine how we felt?

Good fortune was on our side, however, for when we were only a few yards from the lights they changed to amber. The crossing stream of traffic came to a standstill and we shot across unharmed! That is the nearest I have been to heart-failure!

Another exciting experience was broadcasting for the first time. We were with the late Sid Field in a radio show called "Youth Must Have Its Swing"—in 1943. We were almost petrified as we stared at the microphone and realised that millions of people would hear if we made a mistake. But Sid helped us through and everything went off all right.

Oh, and I must tell you about an amusing experience we had once. We arrived at a theatre and the manager, who was standing at the stage door, looked somewhat surprised.

"You are nice and early for the show," he remarked.

"Yes, about two hours," I replied.

The manager grinned.

"A week and two hours!" he corrected.

He was right! Our engagement was for the following week. Were our faces red as we went back to the railway station!

That reminds me of my favourite funny story. It is about a little boy who stood outside the undertaker's, crying his eyes out.

We asked him why he was crying.

"The man in the shop just hit me!" wailed the little lad.

We were just about to inquire into the little lad's distress when the manager of the undertaker's shop came out.

"I'll hit him again if he comes in here ASKING FOR EMPTY BOXES!" he cried. "What does he think this is—a greengrocer's shop?"

Eric Morecambe & Ernie Wise

Picturegoer.

Teaming for Comedy

Focus on fun men: Let's look at filmdom's latest lines in laughter

Hollywood has given us Laurel and Hardy, Abbott and Costello, and Martin and Lewis. These comedy teams have brought pleasure to millions. In Britain we have a team that is delighting music hall audiences: Morecambe and Wise. Some film producer should take a chance on them.—*Edward Brown, 32 Monday Street, Newcastle upon Tyne, 4.*

The Stage

* * *

George and Alfred Black, who present the shows at the Opera House and the Winter Gardens, are still negotiating for stars. Those booked include Ken Platt, Eve Boswell and the Lancashire comedy pair Morecambe and Wise.

* * *

Morecambe and Wise have been re-engaged for John Beaumont's "Babes in the Wood" at Sheffield Lyceum next Christmas. They will be supported by Freddie Sales and Stan Stennett.

Weekly Sporting Review

☆

APOLOGIES are in order to the **Morecambe** and **Wise** team—and their wives! In my story of April 18, I stated that Ernie Wise would become a father in September, whereas, in point of fact, it is Eric Morecambe and his wife, **Joan**, who are the prospective parents. I'm sorry for any embarrassment the juxtaposition (well, that's the right word, isn't it?) may have caused Ernie and **Doreen**, his missus.

Chapter 6

THE ATV YEARS

Ernie: What are you supposed to be?

Eric: I'm a businessman.

Ernie: A businessman doesn't walk like that.

Eric: You don't know my business.

This time Eric and Ernie were determined not to be pushed around, and that meant recruiting their own writers. They opted for SC Green & RM Hills (aka Sid and Dick) who'd written for Arthur Askey and Harry Secombe, but they still had some trouble stamping their authority on the show. Green & Hills were posher than them, and better educated too – and back in 1961, such class distinctions still counted. Eric and Ernie were the stars, but Sid and Dick were the senior partners. They were even on more money – a whopping four hundred quid a week. On television, Sid and Dick were the duo with the track record, not Eric and Ernie. Faced with two rugger playing public schoolboys who'd written for rising stars like Roy Castle and Bruce Forsyth, it's hardly surprising they felt obliged to mind their Ps and Qs.

They felt a lot less reverential after the lukewarm reaction to the first episode. It didn't suffer the same critical mauling as Running Wild, but the response was still pretty tepid. Sid and Dick had filled their sketches with additional characters, and Eric and Ernie felt lost in the crowd. Yet as luck would have it, Equity, the actors union, chose this moment to embark on a bout of industrial action, and most of the actors who'd played these parts promptly went out on strike. As members of a different union, the Variety Artists Federation, Eric and Ernie were free to carry on without

being picketed by militant luvvies, while Sid and Dick were forced to play the supporting roles themselves and write for smaller casts. The strike lasted three months, by which time the first series was finished and a winning formula had been established. After a tricky start, this comic duo had become a quartet.

Eric and Ernie had finally made the giant leap from Variety to TV, and far from cramping their comic style, the small screen made their humour even more intimate. 'Eric's face was made for television,' said Sid. 'He looked so innocent. You could get away with the most outrageous innuendoes when writing for Eric, because nobody believed he was being rude with that face.'[1] Soon they were larking around as if they'd been on telly all their lives. 'It was almost as though they couldn't care less about you, me or the audience,' recalled Sid. 'They were just doing it for themselves.'[2]

Within a few years, The Morecambe & Wise Show had climbed to second spot in the ratings (beaten only by Coronation Street) and their celebrity guests reflected the growing status of the show. In 1964, they played host to the latest pop sensation, the Beatles – though ironically, their producer wanted to get the Fab Four on the show as soon as possible, incase their popularity waned. 'What's it like being famous?' Eric asked John Lennon. 'Well it's not like in your day,' replied Lennon. By now, John, Paul,

George and Ringo were just about the only British stars who could eclipse them.

With the one-eyed god tamed at last, and an award winning show on peak-time telly, their stage work went from strength to strength. 'They were constantly working,' says Joan. 'They never took a holiday.' They played to packed houses in summer season, their pantomimes broke box office records and they topped the bill at the London Palladium – once the pinnacle of their ambitions. It was at the Palladium, in 1964, that they were spotted by Ed Sullivan, compere of America's biggest TV show. Sullivan offered them three guest spots, at $4000 dollars a time. Twenty three years since their first turn together, they'd got their first break in the USA.

For two small town boys who'd been weaned on the escapist Hollywood movies of the Thirties, the United States had always been the Promised Land. 'It was Shangri La to us,' said Ernie. 'We idolised everything about it.' Eric's hero, Stan Laurel, grew up

Left to Right: **Ringo, Paul, George, John, Ernie and Eric. When the Beatles were booked to appear on Eric & Ernie's ATV show in 1964, it was the height of Beatlemania and the studio became a fortress, to protect the Fab Four from their screaming teenage fans. Even so, everyone was entirely unprepared for the mass hysteria that ensued. Eric was quite unnerved by the sheer scale of this adulation, and even wondered whether it was entirely safe to have them on the show.**

in Ulverston, just across the bay from Morecambe, before emigrating to America to establish Hollywood's greatest ever double act. A generation later, could Eric and Ernie do the same?

The first obstacle they had to overcome was their host. The Ed Sullivan show had been going strong since 1948, and now commanded an audience of over fifty million. As a forum for famous entertainers, from Bing Crosby to Elvis Presley, its reputation was unrivalled – yet it was a bit of a mystery how Sullivan had managed to end up as the show's MC. 'He never appeared to do very much,' recollected Eric, 'and even what he did he usually got wrong.'[3] 'Performing was not his strongest asset,' concurs Joan, with considerable understatement. 'In fact, you wondered how on earth he had ever got into show business!'[4] A master of malapropism, Sullivan even struggled with the relatively simple task of bringing on his own guests, introducing Eric and Ernie as 'Morey, Cambey and Wise.' As Eric observed, this left the audience wondering why on earth there were only two of them. No wonder New York wags called it the only live show with a dead host. However despite these considerable handicaps, Eric and Ernie went down pretty well, and over next few years they were invited back several times a year. They also got on well with Sullivan, who despite his limitations as a performer (or in all probability because of them) didn't take himself too seriously. After being billed as a European act (yet another Sullivan faux pas) Eric and Ernie made their next entrance to the rousing strains of Rule Britannia.

Bob Hope said Morecambe & Wise never made it in America because Eric talked too quickly. Another factor may have been that many Americans think too slowly, but the overriding reason was that they didn't put in the hours. They were never going to crack the States without moving there, and though Ernie, with no children to consider, was open to persuasion, Eric was never remotely interested in relocating to the US, either with his family or without them. Their Stateside shows were confined to a series of occasional flying visits, and they were never going to build a US fanbase by performing on TV for just a few minutes at a time. For entertainers with Hollywood ambitions Ed Sullivan was just a springboard, but Eric was always keen to fly straight home again as soon as they'd done their bit. Ernie would always regret that they never gave America their best shot, but Eric's attitude was summed up in his novel Mr Lonely, which he wrote in 1981:

'The only time a British comic does well here is when he plays an upper crust Englishman who talks with a lisp and takes the piss out of himself. Then maybe – and only maybe – he might get by. But stand up

Britain's greatest double act, Morey, Cambey & Wise. Ed Sullivan introduces Eric and Ernie to the American television viewing public.

comics, they started here. This country's had smart arsed comics while England was still laughing at Dan Leno playing a dame in pantomime. You can't compete. What can an Englishman do? First of all they think, "Why is he talking like that?" Then they think, "What's he talking about?" You go out there and mention one English politician and they won't know who you're talking about, including the Prime Minister. There's only one politician you can name, and that's Winston Churchill, and half the audience don't realise he's dead.'[5]

'The difference between American and British show business,' wrote Eric in Mr Lonely, 'was that in Britain you could have a failure and be remembered for your success, while in the States you could have success and be remembered for your failures.'[6] True to form, their final Ed Sullivan appearance, in 1968, was largely ignored by the New York newspapers, and one of the few US papers to acknowledge their existence simply decreed that Morecambe & Wise 'should remain England's problem, not ours.'[6]

In fact the only problem, as far as their transatlantic prospects were concerned, was that they were already doing far too well back in Blighty. In Britain, they were big names at last, after more than twenty years of trying. In America they would have had to begin again from the very bottom, and put their British careers on hold. 'It's taken us years to become stars in this country,' reasoned Eric, when he talked things over with Ernie. 'Do you really want to start all over again over there?' And as Joan observed, prudently, it wasn't wise to be away from Britain for too long, incase they forgot you over here. Ed Sullivan's support was flattering, but Eric was never as keen on Hollywood as Ernie. 'There's only one thing worse than American children in films,' he quipped, 'and that's American grown ups.'

The door to Hollywood remained firmly shut, at least for the time being, yet any disappointment was tempered by the considerable consolation of a movie deal back home. In 1964, Eric and Ernie signed a contract to star in three films for the Rank Organisation, at Pinewood Studios. 'Life's not Hollywood, it's Cricklewood,' Eric never tired of saying. For the next three years Pinewood, not Hollywood, would be the focus of his working life.

Sadly, their film career turned out to be a spectacular disappointment. There wasn't a lot wrong with their performances. In fact, for big screen beginners they seemed remarkably relaxed. Yet none of their directors seemed to know quite what to do with them, and in all three films they came across like two actors from another movie who'd taken a wrong turn in the studio corridor and wandered onto a completely unfamiliar set.

Their first film, The Intelligence Men (released as Spylarks in America) was an awkward spy spoof mainly set in a dreary high rise hotel. Ominously, it was made by the same production team behind the popular but rudimentary Norman Wisdom movies – a detail pounced upon with relish in the film's (mainly withering) reviews. 'An unspeakable British farce in which two funny stage and television comedians are fed through the Norman Wisdom sausage machine,'[7] said The Times. Even worse, the Sun called it 'Bud Abbott and Lou Costello at their worst.' Eric and Ernie had started out aping the broad humour of Abbott & Costello (even recycling some of their material) but it was a style they liked to think they'd long since left behind.

Their second film, That Riviera Touch, at least enjoyed the added perk of a glamorous location. That summer the French Riviera was awash with film crews, and Eric and Ernie hobnobbed with international stars like Tony Curtis and Omar Sharif. Joan joined them in the South of France and had the time of her life. The film didn't

Eric and Ernie embark upon an alternative career as a pair of knitwear models. Thankfully, they never gave up their day jobs.

quite match up to the fun they had making it, but it was certainly a lot better than the one before. Proficiently directed by Cliff Owen, who'd worked with Peter Sellers,[8] it was a complicated crime caper starring Eric and Ernie as British tourists who get caught up in a diamond smuggling racket. Despite a labyrinthine plot, and a distinct shortage of decent gags, the film got better reviews than The Intelligence Men (which wasn't difficult) and did quite well at the box office, in Britain at least. It was still the same uneasy blend of farce and thriller, but at least it played like a proper movie, rather than a string of TV sketches. Eric and Ernie both turned in competent performances, boding well for their next film.

Unfortunately, their third and final Rank movie was even worse than the first one. Eric and Ernie played a pair of hapless travelling salesman who arrive in a South American republic in the middle of a violent civil war. Barry Norman said they seemed strangely inhibited. No wonder, when they were cast adrift in a dog's dinner of a film – part slapstick, part shoot 'em up, a bit like Woody Allen's Bananas, but without the laughs. It was called The Magnificent Two – The Mediocre Two would have been more fitting. In America, it was released as What Happened At Campo Grande (what indeed?), not that many Americans noticed. Though they were creatively disappointing, all three films did reasonably well at the box office, and continue to enjoy healthy sales on video and DVD. However, neither Eric nor Ernie ever really cared for them, and it was obvious to even the most casual Morecambe and Wise fan that they were capable of so much more. Eric didn't suffer from false modesty, and always loved watching his best shows on television. Yet he was an astute critic of his weaker work, and it was telling that when one of his feature films was shown on TV, he would switch off the set. 'If we had Neil Simon writing for us and Billy Wilder directing, I know we could be international stars,'[9] reflected Eric, ruefully. He might have been right, but sadly they never got another chance.

Eric and Ernie at Pinewood Studios, filming their last film for the Rank Organisation, The Magnificent Two.

Below: **Eric and Ernie collect yet another award. By now, Eric's house was so full of them that he gave this one to his mum. She put it ontop of the telly, where it remained for several years until it mysteriously toppled over and snapped in half during a broadcast by Uri Geller. Eric's mum Sadie swore that Geller's paranormal powers were responsible for the breakage.**

Tommy Cooper (far left) makes Ernie fall about, while Eric picks his pocket.

"Evening Standard"

"Sunday Pictorial"

STARLESS

☆ THERE'S one thing you'll never get out of the B.B.C.—the names of the artists who are going to be built up.

The smallest film company is prepared to herald its new names for 1954. But the B.B.C. just zips its lips and hopes that old Joe Public will make the stars for it.

Here are five new names that have come up in the past six months. All have a quality which might be star material. But it needs grooming, sifting, producing. First **Morecambe and Wise**, comedians. They've got youth and a zany line in patter, but they lack polish and ease of presentation. They need a producer to develop their individual personalities.

Sally Barnes, a girl with a real gift for comedy and pathos. But she must get new material to take her out of the charlady belt.

Shirley Abicair. The most natural discovery of 1953. She's the eternal girl next door that every young man wants to marry. But she's not a solo artist. She needs a show to bring out the warmth of her personality.

Mary Millar. A sweet little voice. A fragile beauty. Is she to remain just a singer or has she dramatic qualities that haven't been explored so far?

. . . **Morecambe and Wise**, TV comics named by me last week, get their own series in April. . . .

Would you laugh at these?

Morecambe and Wise.

I SAY YES!

by George Campey

IF any names are found on the heart of television's light entertainment boss, Ronald Waldman, they are likely to be those of Norman Wisdom, Arthur Askey and Richard Hearne.

These are his stalwarts in the field of television comedy. I enjoy each one. But is it not time that Mr. Waldman was thinking beyond this triumvirate?

None of the three is able to do much television nowadays. And television badly needs a new comedy series.

Now I don't want to hear any moans from Mr. Waldman and his henchmen about not being able to find the artists, because I have found them. Their names are Eric Bartholomew and Ernest Wiseman.

Crazy comedy

Mr. Waldman and his customers on this side of the screen will know them better as Morecambe and Wise.

These young comedians have been seen on the TV screen three times. They will be seen again in a brief act on December 12.

I hope Mr. Waldman is there with a dotted line for Messrs. Morecambe and Wise to sign on. For I count these two men the white hopes of television humour. Theirs is crazy comedy which owes something to Hellzapoppin and the Marx Brothers.

It is polished, and fast.

Morecambe (he took the name of his home town) and Yorkshireman Wise are both 27. They were "discoveries" of Brian Michie in 1939.

They went on tour at a salary of £5 a week each. "And," says Morecambe, "I used to send money home out of that." Came the call-up. Morecambe went into the mines, Wise into the Merchant Navy. They teamed up again after the war. Now they top the bill at provincial variety theatres.

£150 a week

Would they leave the music hall for the fickle world of television? I can tell Mr. Waldman that they would. "There is nobody making a mark on television now," says Morecambe. "We would like to try—especially after the fan-mail we received on our last television appearances."

Both Morecambe and Wise were surprised at the favourable reaction of viewers.

Perhaps Mr. Waldman is worried about money? I can report that Morecambe and Wise are making £150 a week. Television could run to that at least—if it sincerely wants new faces and new talent as much as the viewers do.

Mr. Waldman is on his way back from chasing programme ideas through the American TV jungle. Having found him two white hopes in his absence, all he needs to do now is to act.

"Evening Chronicle"

Radio and TV . . . By Malcolm Moore

On the Way Up

They're in Henry Hall's TV show tonight.

THERE is a strong possibility that the North's latest and snappiest comedy stars, Morecambe and Wise, will be established television favourites by this time next year.

They tell me that Ronnie Waldman, TV's light entertainment chief, has approached them regarding a show in the New Year, and they are busy "thinking up some ideas."

Their names have leapt to the front in the past few weeks as stars of that new topical Northern radio show with the slick line of patter, "You're Only Young Once."

Ernie Wise says they would like to see the show on the Light Programme, and kept there by the quality of its humour. Candidly, I feel they have made a good start on the way in the hands of producer Ronnie Taylor—and they think so too.

Tonight Morecambe and Wise "Face The Music" in Henry Hall's TV show. This is not their first television appearance, and certainly not their last.

Youth is on their side, Eric Morecambe, war-time Lancashire Bevin boy, is only 27, and ex-Merchant Navy Ernie Wise his senior by a year.

But the secret of their success is that they have been a team 14 years already, for they paired up when still at school. Eric (otherwise John Eric Bartholomew) adopted the name of his own town—Morecambe—while Ernie shortened his surname from Wiseman to Wise. He comes from Leeds.

Talent spotter Bryan Michie set them on the road to the top as two of his discoveries.

Keep it up, boys!

Eric at Pinewood Studios filming The Magnificent Two in 1967.

Chapter 7

Keep Going, You Fool!

✷

Ernie: When will this torture end?

Eric: I don't know. What time does the curtain come down?

After failing to break into movies on either side of the Atlantic, Eric and Ernie could have been forgiven for settling for a profitable but pedestrian TV career. They weren't short of money and they deserved a chance to put their feet up. Yet though their act harked back to music hall, they were always on the look out for the next big thing, and the way they went about the business side of things was always bang up to date. Far earlier than most comedians, they'd realised Variety's days were numbered, and had made the great escape to TV while a lot of other comics went down with the ship. 'I won't believe in colour TV until I see it in black and white,' they used to joke, but now that TV was established, they could see colour was the coming thing, so in 1968 they asked Lew Grade, head of ATV (and the closest thing in Britain to a genuine screen mogul) when they could stop doing their show in boring old black and white. 'You'll have colour when I say you have colour,'[1] he replied.

Most entertainers would have left it at that. After all, this cigar chomping TV magnate had kept them on peaktime telly for the best part of a decade. He'd even sold two million quid's worth of their ATV shows (in colour) to the US. Yet Eric and Ernie were a lot more far sighted than most entertainers, so after seven successful years at ATV, they started to scout around for other offers – which is how Billy Marsh's partner, Michael Grade (who just so happened to be Lew Grade's nephew) came to put in a call to Bill Cotton Junior, Head of Variety at the BBC. 'Are you interested in Morecambe & Wise?' asked Grade. Of course he was. 'They have not come to an agreement with Lew and we are making enquiries for an alternative source of employment,' explained Grade. 'Stay where you are,' said Cotton. 'I'm coming up.'[2]

Eric and Ernie joined the BBC, bringing Sid and Dick with them, and Cotton wasted no time finding the right person to oversee their new show, collaring seasoned TV producer John Ammonds in the BBC club bar. 'How would you like to produce Morecambe & Wise?' asked Cotton. 'You'll never get them,' said Ammonds, who was about to go on holiday. 'They're with Lew Grade over at ATV.' 'I've got them,'[3] said Cotton. It was the chance of a lifetime. Ammonds cancelled his holiday and set to work.

Ammonds had worked with Eric and Ernie years before, on their radio show, You're Only Young Once, and now he helped them bridge the gap between Variety and TV. On the one hand, he preserved the old music hall ambience of their act, filming them on a raised stage, complete with wings and curtain, and featuring old colleagues like Arthur Tolcher in a variety of supporting roles. Yet although the appearance of the show was reassuringly traditional, its production techniques were thoroughly modern. Ammonds used lots of close ups and reaction shots, so Eric could confide in the viewers, and draw

them in. 'Eric used the camera so well,' says his son, Gary. 'People came to love him for all those little touches.' But it took Ammonds to bring them out. Recordings began in August, but there was no let up once the series ended. After the last show went out in October, Eric and Ernie packed their bags and headed off for a fortnight at Batley Variety Club.

Above: **Eric with Peter Haigh, a BBC presenter who'd retired to Portugal. Haigh presented Come Dancing, and the BBC's pioneering cinema series, Picture Parade.**

Looking back, it was clearly an accident waiting to happen, although nobody could possibly have predicted it at the time. Spurred on by his mother, and haunted by the inherent insecurity of show business, for thirty years Eric had been pushing himself far too hard. It was a hard slog for Ernie too, but he was far better at handling it. 'I'm an optimist,' Ernie used to say. 'I get up in the same mood as I went to bed.'[4] 'Anything that came along, they had to grab it,' says Joan, but Ernie was a lot better at letting go.

Eric, on the other hand, found it practically impossible to unwind. 'Even having twenty minutes at home putting his feet up on the sofa he would regard as boredom,' says Gary. 'He felt that he should be permanently working to keep the Morecambe & Wise machine going.' Even when Joan persuaded him to take a break, and retreat to their villa in the Algarve, he carried on working. 'He was never willing to let go,' says Gary. 'He didn't really know what a holiday was.' While Joan took the kids to the beach, he'd sit on the veranda, tapping away at the typewriter. 'I've got a brilliant idea for the Christmas show!' he'd say, when she got back. 'But it's only September!' Joan would tell him. 'I don't think he ever completely left the show behind,' she says. 'He was always thinking about the show.'

Even Eric's own idea of R&R was hardly what the rest of us would call low key. In the evenings, in foreign restaurants, he'd entertain the waiters, though they often had no idea who he was. Even on the plane he would frequently lark around. 'In the unlikely event of this plane reaching Portugal, we hope you have a pleasant stay,' he would announce to his fellow passengers. 'Due to unforeseen circumstances, we are now flying at an altitude of three feet.'[5] Back home it was the same story. With close friends or complete strangers, he felt the same constant compulsion to perform. When workmen came to build a swimming pool in his garden, Eric came out to film them dressed as a silent movie director, in a peaked cap and plus fours.

Ernie was the tortoise, Eric was the hare, but it wasn't just their personalities that made a difference – it was their job descriptions, too. As the straight man, Ernie could afford to switch off once the cameras stopped rolling, but as the comic turn, the creative force, Eric found it far harder to wind down. After every show, there'd be a backstage party, and while Ernie usually turned in fairly early, Eric would always be among the last to leave. He was drinking more than he used to ('I gargle with whisky, and I'm afraid some of it slips down') and smoking at least sixty fags a day. 'And that was before I started on my own,' he said, but it was no laughing matter. 'Eric's health was never good,' said Ernie. 'He never did look terribly well.'[6]

Now they were stars, the phone never stopped ringing, yet after all the lean years, when bookings were so hard to come by, they hated to turn anything down. At Batley, they did over an hour every night, at midnight, including several dance routines and acrobatic falls. After Batley, they were booked to play a New York nightclub, the Royal Variety Show, and then eight weeks in panto. Worried that this lucrative work might soon dry up forever, instead of sitting back and enjoying the fruits of their success they were working even harder than they'd ever done before.

Throughout the first week at Batley, Eric had a strange pain in his arm. He thought it must be rheumatism or maybe tennis elbow, but as the week wore on he felt worse and worse. 'Let's get off,' he told Ernie on Thursday. 'Let's keep it short.'[7] He soldiered on until the finale, but as soon as the curtain fell, he left Ernie signing autographs and headed straight back to his hotel. However Eric's hotel was nearly thirty miles away, and one of his colleagues at the club suggested it might be best to drive back through Leeds, rather than travelling cross country. It was a piece of advice that quite possibly saved his life. By the time he reached Leeds, the pain had spread to his chest. 'I didn't know what was happening,' he recalled. 'I thought I'd got my braces twisted at the back.'[8] But deep down, he knew it was much more serious than that. He didn't know it yet, but he was having a heart attack. He stopped the car, unable to drive any further, wound down the window and sat there waiting, hoping a Good Samaritan might pass by before he died.

That Good Samaritan was a man called Walter Butterworth, and although he undoubtedly saved Eric's life, he managed to do it in a manner that wouldn't have looked out of place in one of Eric's routines. 'Could you direct me to the nearest hospital?' asked Eric, but Walter's directions were hopeless. 'Look, I don't feel very well,' interjected Eric. 'Could you possibly drive me there?' 'I'm in the Territorials,' said Walter. 'I've only driven a tank.'[9] The first hospital they found had no Accident & Emergency. At the second one, Walter left Eric in the car while he went to find a wheelchair. Eventually, Eric got out and walked into hospital himself. 'Look, my mates at work will never believe me,' said Walter, as Eric was wheeled down the hospital corridor. 'Do me a favour. Before you go, could you sign this for me?'[10] Eric scribbled an autograph for Walter, convinced it would be his last.

Back in Harpenden, Joan was woken in the small hours by a call from the hospital, summoning her to her husband's bedside. 'I thought someone was playing some sort of terrible joke,' she says, but the hospital brought her to her senses. 'You'd better hurry up,' they told her, 'or you may be too late.'[11] Joan's stomach turned over. Until that

Above: **Eric supports the nurses.**

Below: **Eric in Leeds Infirmary, with Joan, after his first heart attack, in 1968. From the brave face they both put on for the cameras, you'd never guess that Eric had nearly died a few days before.**

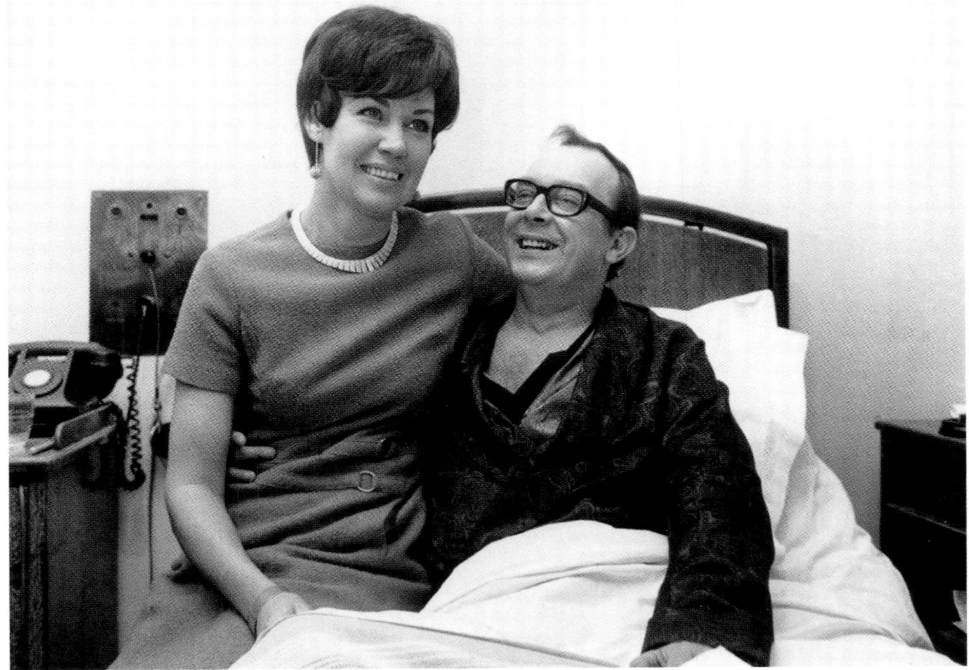

Above: **Eric enjoys a fag break with his mum and dad, George and Sadie, back in the good old days before cigarettes were bad for you.**

Below: **Eric & Ernie's writers, Sid Green and Dick Hills, sent this tongue in cheek get well telegram to Eric after his first heart attack. Shortly after this, Sid and Dick left Eric & Ernie for alternative employment at ATV, assuming that Eric might never be fit enough to work again.**

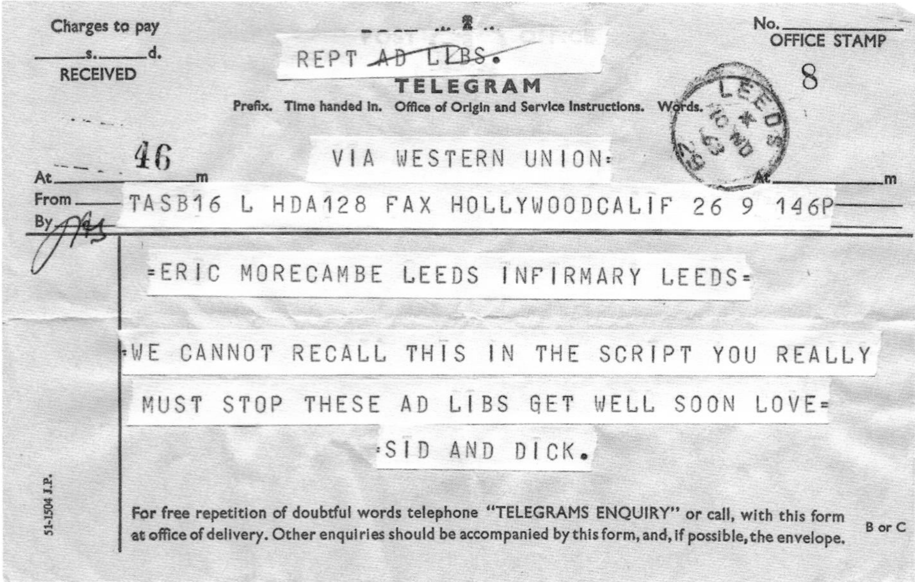

Charges to pay
s. d.
RECEIVED

REPT ~~AD LIBS~~.

TELEGRAM

Prefix. Time handed in. Office of Origin and Service Instructions. Words.

No.
OFFICE STAMP
8

46

At m

VIA WESTERN UNION=

At m

From TASB16 L HDA128 FAX HOLLYWOODCALIF 26 9 146P

By

=ERIC MORECAMBE LEEDS INFIRMARY LEEDS=

=WE CANNOT RECALL THIS IN THE SCRIPT YOU REALLY MUST STOP THESE AD LIBS GET WELL SOON LOVE=

=SID AND DICK.

51-1504 J.P.

For free repetition of doubtful words telephone "TELEGRAMS ENQUIRY" or call, with this form at office of delivery. Other enquiries should be accompanied by this form, and, if possible, the envelope.

B or C

moment, she'd never considered he might die. She hurried up to Leeds where she found Eric in an oxygen tent. Even in his plastic cocoon, he could see she was upset. 'I'm going to be all right, you know, love,' he reassured her. 'I'm not going to die,'[12] yet the doctors warned her that the next 48 hours would be crucial. 'You'll do anything for a laugh,'[13] quipped Ernie when he came to visit, but he was in tears on the way out. In Paignton, Des O'Connor stopped his show to make a special announcement. 'Will you do something for me?' O'Connor asked his audience. 'Would you say a prayer for Eric Morecambe tonight, because he's fighting for his life.' 'Well,' said Eric, when the news of O'Connor's valiant attempt at faith healing finally got back to him, 'those six or seven people probably made all the difference.'[14] Eric was still as funny as ever, but at 42, nobody knew whether he would ever work again.

For the time being, however, work was the last thing on his mind. 'For the first time, he was conscious that there was another world out there, outside of Morecambe & Wise,' says Gary. Never again would Eric complain that he was bored. He was ordered to take three months off. He decided to take six, since he reckoned his job was probably twice as stressful as the average occupation. It was probably an underestimate. Eric always said comedy was based on fear, but this fear was of a different kind. 'He lost a lot of confidence,' says Joan. 'He was frightened of going back to work.'

Eric and Ernie's second series for the BBC was postponed indefinitely, but loyal to the last, Ernie refused to work without him, even turning down an invitation to do a solo spot at the London Palladium. Greater love hath no comedian... He did allow himself a few personal appearances, but even then he still sent Eric half his personal appearance fees. Keen to keep busy, Ernie flew to New York, to try and sell some Morecambe & Wise shows to Ed Sullivan, and flying back via Barbados, he heard from an airline steward that Sid and Dick had returned to ATV. Ernie knew nothing about it, but it was already in all the papers. He wasn't best pleased to be the last to know. Back in England, Eric heard the news from a reporter who phoned him for a quote. 'Eric and Ernie were so hurt because Sid and Dick wrote them off,' says Joan, but she could see Sid and Dick's point of view. Lew Grade had told them Eric wouldn't be back for a year, and in the meantime, they had to make a living. It was the fact that the story broke before they told Eric and Ernie that really hurt. 'Eric never forgave them,' says Gary, but this incident, though painful, proved to be a blessing, since it opened the door for a writer who took their comedy to a completely different level.

Above: **Spot the difference. Eric and Ernie pose alongside their waxworks at Madame Tussauds. In fact, Eric thought his waxwork looked more like TV presenter Cliff Michelmore. Ernie, on the other hand, thought his looked more like Fred Flinstone's straight man, Barney Rubble.**

Right: **Eric and Ernie switch on the lights in Morecambe.**

Above: **Eric with Formula One champion Graham Hill. They became close friends during the early 1970s. Sadly, their friendship was cut short when Graham died in an air crash in 1975, while piloting his own plane.**

Below: **Eric's first flash car, a Jensen Interceptor.**

Chapter 8

The BBC Years

Andre Previn: You're playing all the wrong notes.

Eric: I'm playing all the right notes, but not necessarily in the right order.

Unlike most people in Britain in 1969, Eddie Braben wasn't a Morecambe & Wise fan. He'd seen them years before, as young unknowns, at the Liverpool Empire. 'They were so far down the bill,' he says, 'I thought they were the printers.' They were still aping Abbott & Costello back then, and Braben was unimpressed. 'They really had no set act,' he says. 'It was just a hotchpotch of gags.' By 1969, they'd become household

names, but although he'd seen them on TV, Braben still hadn't warmed to them. 'They were topping bills all over the country,' he says, 'but I didn't like them. I thought Ernie was too abrasive. I thought he was too hard. And I thought Eric was silly – rather George Formby silly, without the George Formby charm.' And so when Bill Cotton rang him and asked if he'd like to write for them, he didn't think it would work. Braben said no, but Cotton was insistent. 'Come down and meet the boys,'1 he said. Against his better instincts, Braben went.

Braben had started writing gags while working as a greengrocer (and hating every second of it) on a fruit and veg stall in his native Liverpool. 'I used to write about 3000 jokes a week and they were 3000 of the worst jokes you've ever read in your life.'[2] He sold his first joke to Charlie Chester for two and six: 'When he was a little baby, Hopalong Cassidy's mother knew he was going to be a cowboy because he always wore a ten gallon nappy.' If that was one of the better ones, can you imagine what the worst ones were like? In his first year, he earned less than 30 shillings, but by the time Cotton called him up, he'd become one of the best gagsmiths in the country. For the last fourteen years, he'd been writing for fellow Liverpudlian Ken Dodd. 'If he writes as well for us,' said Eric, 'the answer must be yes.'[2] However Dodd was a pure stand up comic, who only really did one liners. 'I'm only a gag man,' Braben warned them. 'I've never done situations.' 'If you can write original jokes,' said Eric, 'you can write original sketches.'[3] 'We'll suggest a few ideas,' said Cotton, 'and you go away and write the boys a show.'[4]

Despite his initial reservations, Braben returned home inspired. When he met Eric and Ernie face to face, he found he liked them both enormously. He also witnessed an intimacy between them that he'd never seen on TV. 'They were closer than any two brothers I've ever met.' 'Why haven't I seen this in their performances?' he wondered, on the train back to Liverpool. 'Why have I only seen the harsh, hard side? Why haven't I seen the love that exists between these two men?' 'Get that love and affection across to an audience and you're half way home,'[5] he thought.

After a frantic week's writing, Braben returned to London with his first ever Morecambe & Wise script. Eric and Ernie loved it, but they weren't sure they could do it justice. 'They liked it very, very much but they both said it wasn't for them because they'd never worked like this before,' says Braben. 'In fact, they'd never had a script that was written from the beginning to the end.' Hills and Green used to turn up with a few rough ideas, and flesh them out as they went along. But Cotton was convinced this new approach would work, and having found Braben's script so funny, Eric and Ernie didn't need a great deal of persuading. Britain's best double act had become a trio.

In the summer of 1969, Eric and Ernie returned to the studio for their first time since Eric's heart attack. The tension in the audience was palpable, but Eric broke the ice by peering inside his jacket and muttering, 'Keep going, you fool!' It was a masterstroke by Eric, and by Eddie Braben. As Eric said of Ernie's hairline, you couldn't see the join. Their first live show, a few months later, got a five minute standing ovation. Eric and Ernie were back, and with Ammonds and Braben on board, they were better than ever.

Mindful of Eric's state of health, Cotton allowed them three weeks to rehearse each episode, and this extra preparation gave these new shows added zip. Eric and Ernie soon settled into a prosaic yet highly productive schedule. Every day, at 10am precisely, their respective Rolls Royces would drop them off at the North Kensington Community Centre on Dalgarno Way, a broken bottle's throw from Wormwood Scrubs. 'You've never seen a more grotty place in all your life,' says Eric's chauffeur, Mike Fountain. 'There was one telephone, in the office. That was the only contact you

Left to Right: **Robert Morley, Eric, Ernie. Unimpressed with Eric & Ernie's Spartan catering arrangements (a cup of homemade pea soup from a thermos flask) Morley sent out for a Fortnum & Mason's hamper. Though they were renowned workaholics, and rarely took a proper lunch break, Eric & Ernie made an exception in this case, and took four hours off to demolish it.**

had with outside world.' Free from outside interruptions, they'd rehearse all day, pausing only for a few sandwiches and a mug of Eric's homemade pea and ham soup –'thick enough to trot a donkey across,'[6] said Eric.

Robert Morley was unimpressed with this primitive repast (he sent out for a Fortnum & Mason's hamper) but like most of their guests, he was extremely impressed by their work rate. Only amateurs can afford the luxury of an artistic temperament, and there was nothing starry about the BBC's brightest stars. Rehearsals were meticulously thorough (there really was no other way to create the show's air of carefully contrived chaos) and visiting celebrities were reassured that they would never be made to look foolish, even when they were required to play the fool.

'The guests always had a ball,' says Joan, and so did the studio audience. 'Those early shows were just staggering. They were like first nights.' It felt more like being at a West End show than a conventional TV recording, and the studio looked a lot like a West End theatre, too. 'They had curtains that opened and closed, just like in the music hall,' says

Braben. 'It created a wonderful, warm atmosphere, rather than the clinical operating theatre feeling that you get in television studios.'

Peter Cushing was their first star guest, playing King Arthur in a Camelot skit (returning in subsequent episodes to pester them for his unpaid appearance fee), followed by every sort of celebrity, from posh actors like Michael Redgrave to pop singers like Nana Mouskouri. However it wasn't just the famous guests that made the new Morecambe & Wise Show so special. Above all, it was the way Braben rejigged the relationship between Morecambe and Wise. Until now they'd been a conventional double act, with Eric as the comic and Ernie as his stooge. Braben made Eric smarter, more like Eric's American idol, Phil Silvers, and he made Ernie more pompous, giving him a lot more laughs. Ernie was recast as a prolifically awful (yet absurdly self-important) playwright, churning out several dreadful new dramas every day. 'At last I have a character,' Ernie told Braben, full of gratitude for his new role. 'I'm not just standing there saying, "What did you do?" "What did you say?" I have something I can perform.' For the first time, he wasn't just a feed but a proper comic, with punchlines of his own. 'You could be another Brontë sister,' Eric would tell him. 'But I can't sing,' Ernie would reply.

Where's my fee? Left to Right: **Eric, Peter Cushing, Ernie. Cushing, a great sport, was Eric & Ernie's first major guest star, in an age when 'serious' actors rarely demeaned themselves by appearing with comedians.**

'Eric was grateful too because it gave him something to bounce off,' says Braben. Eric was now recast as Ernie's shrewd but idle flatmate – a canny layabout well aware that Ernie was a useless writer yet fiercely protective of him all the same. 'I told you he could write,' he'd say, after asking Ernie for his autograph. The old Eric was a fool, the new Eric merely played the fool, and this development opened up a wealth of untapped comic possibilities. 'I showed this enormous love and friendship that existed between the two of them,' says Braben, 'and the audience could see it as well.'

Like their heroes, Laurel & Hardy, Braben even persuaded them to share a bed, though Eric always smoked his pipe, so he didn't look too camp. 'Pipe smoking and homosexuality just don't seem to blend,'[7] he said. He needn't have worried. Braben had created a situation comedy cunningly disguised as a vaudeville show, and as in all good sitcoms, the audience found it easy to suspend their disbelief. 'The thinking behind placing Eric and Ernie in a double bed was simply that there was no escape,' explains Braben. 'They could speak their innermost thoughts, taunt, jibe and insult each other, something that they would never, ever do in front of anyone else.'[8] John Mortimer was quite right to liken their partnership to an English marriage, 'missing out the sex, as many English marriages do.'[9]

By 1973, Eric's star had risen so high that he was profiled in The Observer by Britain's foremost theatre critic and cultural commentator, Kenneth Tynan – a remarkable accolade, since in those days comics were rarely treated as proper artists, worthy of proper criticism or praise. 'There comes a point at which sheer professional skill, raised to the highest degree by the refining drudgery of constant practice, evolves into something different in kind,' wrote Tynan, in his florid prose, 'conferring on its possessors an assurance that enables them to take off, to ignite, to achieve outrageous feats of timing and audience control that would, even a few years before, have been beyond them.'[10] What Tynan was trying to say (I think) was that an act which had previously been very good had suddenly become quite brilliant. Tynan was the first to articulate this fact, but he was hardly the first to spot it. For anyone who owned a television set, the change was plain to see.

Stars queued up to appear with them, even though they always got a hearty ribbing. 'I didn't come here to be insulted,' said Robin Day. 'Where do you usually go?' asked Eric. Yehudi Menuhin was told to bring his banjo and Rudolf Nureyev was requested to fill in for Lionel Blair, yet appearing on the show actually enhanced their celebrity status. As Roy Castle said, it was an honour to be abused by Eric and Ernie. It was a good career move, too. Hollywood writer, producer and director Melvin Frank saw Glenda Jackson horsing around with Eric and Ernie and offered her a role in his film,

This page: **Ernie, Glenda and Eric.**

Left: **Stick with us, kid, and you'll get an Oscar. Eric & Ernie enjoy a toga party with Glenda Jackson, future Labour MP for Hampstead & Highgate.**

'I'm playing all the right notes, but not necessarily in the right order.' Left to Right: **Eric, Andre Previn and Ernie. Victoria Wood called this the greatest comedy sketch of all time.**

A Touch of Class, which won her an Oscar. Eric and Ernie sent her a telegram. 'Stick with us, kid,' it read, 'and you'll get another.' Sure enough, she went back on the Morecambe & Wise Show and won a second Academy Award. Yet the finest comic performance didn't come from a classical actor but from a classical conductor. Andre Previn had to break off rehearsals with Eric and Ernie to fly home to see his sick mother in America, and only arrived back in Britain the day before the show. He learnt the script in the cab from the airport, but as befits a great musician, his timing was perfect. As Eric said, 'it turned out to be one of the best sketches we've ever done.'[11]

In 1974, John Ammonds stepped down and Ernest Maxin replaced him, yet far from winding down, Eric and Ernie found another gear. A former child performer, and a producer of the Black & White Minstrel Show, Maxin was an old fashioned song and dance man through and through, and he brought a touch of MGM glamour to Morecambe & Wise. No expense was spared – his sets and costumes were always sumptuous. He even used proper tracking shots, a big screen technique rarely lavished on British TV. His heroes were vintage showmen like Gene Kelly and Fred Astaire, and he recreated the same razzamatazz on the small screen, staging lush production numbers like Eric and Ernie's bone dry rendition of Singin' In The Rain – a Gene Kelly pastiche that was immaculate in every detail, apart from a complete absence of rain. Like all the best spoofs, it was motivated by deep affection. For Eric and Ernie, who'd been raised on films like these in the flea pit cinemas of Leeds and Morecambe, this was a comic dream come true.

Maxin's finest hour came in the 1976 Christmas Show, when he cast Angela Rippon in a high kicking Broadway number. Maxin got the idea when he bumped into Rippon in the BBC studios. It was the first time he'd seen her from the waist down. Wrapped in a tight skirt, he was struck by her beauty, and in particular her lovely long legs – legs that remained hidden beneath a desk when she read the Nine O'Clock News. 'Would you like to sing?' he asked her. 'I don't think so,' she said. 'I'd probably clear the studio.'[12] Maxin asked if she could dance. Yes, said Rippon, she could.

When Eric met Rippon, he saw what Maxin was on about. 'Do you do anything else other than read the news?' he asked her. 'Well, I used to be a ballet dancer,'[13] she replied, and a classic dance routine was born. Rippon went back to her old ballet teacher for a month's rigorous refresher course, and her performance was a sensation – in those days, newsreaders rarely did anything else but read the news. 'What colour

The Avengers. Eric rebuffs the amorous advances of Diana Rigg's Nell Gwyn.

are her eyes?' Eric asked the warm up man afterwards. 'I don't know,' he replied. 'No, you dirty little devil,' said Eric. 'You were looking at her legs![14] As were we all. 'I don't think a week goes by when someone doesn't come up to me and mention the show,'[15] reflected Rippon, nearly twenty years later. Nearly thirty years on, it's still the thing about her that most of us remember best.

In 1976, Eric and Ernie were both awarded the OBE. 'All this fuss and I'm only a clown,'[16] said Eric, but secretly he was delighted. 'I'll wear it on state occasions,' he said, 'like Luton Town home games.'[17] Even outside Buckingham Palace, Eric couldn't resist larking around. In press photos of the pair, Ernie is holding up his medal for the photographers. Eric, on the other hand, is holding up his wristwatch. 'Thank you very much for all the happiness that you've given the people,' said the Queen.

In one respect, at least, Eric and Ernie had already upstaged their monarch. Even more than the Queen's Speech, the Morecambe & Wise Christmas Show had become the televisual event of the festive season, as integral as turkey and plum pudding, said Ernie – and he wasn't the only one who thought so. 'Journalists were sneaking in photographers to get snapshots of whoever was going to be in the show, so they could leak it to the tabloids,' recalls Gary. If people didn't like the Morecambe & Wise Christmas Show, they felt they'd had a bad Christmas, and so five weeks rehearsal were given over to getting it absolutely right. 'They had a terrible lot to live up to, and I think that did become extremely stressful for Eric,' explains Joan. 'Ernie was always more laid back about it. With Eric it wasn't the money, it was the standard – to keep the standard up, to come up with the goods, to come up with new ideas. That always drove him. That drove him all his life.'

In 1977, Eric and Ernie didn't even do a series. They devoted all their attention to the Christmas Show, compiling a guest list that included Penelope Keith, Paul Eddington, Arthur Lowe and Elton John. The piece de resistance was a rendition of There Is Nothing Like A Dame (from the musical South Pacific) sung by a troupe of somersaulting TV presenters, including Michael Aspel, Richard Baker, Frank Bough and Barry Norman. 'What struck me was their consummate professionalism,' remembers Norman. 'When the work started, the larking about stopped. They didn't waste time and they were amazingly patient with us blundering amateurs in the chorus, but they were quietly insistent that everything should be done right.'[18] All that hard work paid off. Nearly twenty nine million people saw the show – more than half the population, and over six million more than the audience for the Queen's Speech. For Eric and Ernie, the future possibilities seemed infinite. 'By the mid Seventies, I was

London Weekend Television
South Bank Television Centre, Kent House, Upper Ground, London SE1 9LT. (Registered Office)
Telex: 918123. Cables: Weekendtel London SE1. PBX Telephone: 01-261 3434.

Direct Line: 01-261 - 3060

Eric Morecambe & Ernie Wise,
"Bracefield",
Redborn Lane,
Harpenden,
Herts.

15th June '76

Dear Eric & Ernie

Many many congratulations on your recognition in the Birthday Honours list - definitely not before time. You must both be highly delighted. Under the heading "For services to the entertainment industry" do I take it this is really a reward for all your work for the S.T.P.F.D.B.O.C. one of the most worthwhile causes (save the public from Desmond Bernard O'Connor).

By the way even though you two no doubt made a big hole in our Saturday audience, it was marvellous to see the christmas show again.

With all best wishes for your continued success.

Yours sincerely,

Michael

Michael Grade (C.T.T.S.)*

* Crawler to the Stars!

London Weekend Television Limited. Registered in England (No. 908673)
Directors: John Freeman CHAIRMAN & CHIEF EXECUTIVE Lord Hartwell DEPUTY CHAIRMAN Brian Tesler DEPUTY CHIEF EXECUTIVE Vic Gardiner GENERAL MANAGER
Cyril Bennett CONTROLLER OF PROGRAMMES Ron Miller SALES DIRECTOR Peter McNally FINANCIAL CONTROLLER The Hon. David Astor, Robert Clark
G. H. Ross Goobey, H. C. Hardy, Duncan McNab, The Hon. David Montagu, Evelyn de Rothschild.

absolutely convinced it would last forever,' says Gary. 'Eric wasn't. He was still waiting for it all to be taken away. He was still stashing away money for that rainy day.' But come rain or shine, nobody could have predicted what would happen next. Barely a month after that record breaking Christmas show, Eric and Ernie dropped their bombshell. They were leaving the BBC.

spike milligan

9 Orme Court,
London, W.2.

6th January 1976

Messrs E. Morecombe and E. Wise,
Brachefield,
Red Bourne Lane,
Herts.

Dear Lads,

Re grinning Des O'Connor on your Programme. You missed out the greatest squelcher line when he said:

"Can I sing on your Show?"

The answer was:

"Sing on our Show? You can't sing on your own Show".

Thought you ought to know.

Love, Light and Peace,

Spike

Spike Milligan

Eric and his piano playing protégé, Reg Dwight. They became firm friends, despite their rival footballing affiliations – Elton John was the Chairman of Watford FC, Eric was a director of Luton Town.

Above. Left to Right: **Ernie, Penelope Keith, Eric.** Below. **The Young Ones.** Left to Right: **Cliff Richard, Ernie, Eric.**

Above: **Eric and Ernie film an advert for WH Smith. Eric's funniest ad libs often ended up on the cutting room floor.**

Eric shares a jokes with the king and queen of holiday camps, Sir Billy and Lady Butlin.

Eric at his daughter Gail's wedding, 1975. The father of the bride is leaning on a walking stick, since he'd had a small brain spasm that morning, and could hardly get out of bed.

Above: **Eric at daughter Gail's wedding, 1975.**

Right: **On the patio at Eric's villa in Portugal, where many great sketches were written, including the celebrated Shirley Bassey routine.** Left to right: **daughter Gail, Eric, son Gary.**

Eric and Joan at a private party.

THE
MORECAMBE &
WISE SHOW

THE
GOLDEN
ROSE
OF
MONTREUX

1970

QE2 Cruise, 1971.
Right: **Western Night – Eric as Wyatt Earp.**
Below: **Eric does his favourite sight gag: 'If it's the Invisible Man, tell him I can't see him'.**

Chapter 9

The Thames Years

Ernie: The worst thing you can do to the public has always been to bore them. If you bore them you shouldn't be there.

Eric: I think it's time we left.

'**Morecambe & Wise** quitting BBC for ITV,' 1 read the banner headline across the front page of the London Evening Standard. All the other papers swiftly followed suit. Two comedians negotiate new contract with rival TV channel – not such a big story, you might have thought – but Eric and Ernie were now a national institution. It was like ITV snapping up the rights to the FA Cup, the Boat Race AND the Grand National. For Bill Cotton, it felt like a divorce, and even though most people didn't take it quite so personally, it was still a very surprising (if not downright shocking) piece of news.

So why did Eric and Ernie abandon Auntie Beeb? Ernie said it was for the money, but although ITV offered them five times as much, the BBC matched it – and still they went. The real reason was the promise of another movie. Unlike the BBC, ITV's London flagship, Thames TV, had its own film company, Euston Films, a company which Eric and Ernie thought would revive their film careers. 'Those three films weren't much good,' said Eric, recalling their mediocre Rank movies, 'but we had always hoped to do more.'[2] Rather than stay with the BBC, and pursue an independent film deal, they decided that Thames, and Euston Films, was their main chance.

'Eric had a burning ambition to do a film,' says Joan. 'It was never, ever just the money.' Gary agrees. 'Ever since the Sixties, Eric and Ernie had both wanted to make a big film,' he confirms. 'Ernie because he still dreamt of Hollywood, and being a big film star – which is a bit sad, but there you go – and Eric – which is also sad – because he wanted to do something like Peter Sellers' Pink Panther, and they hadn't achieved that with Rank. The Rank films had been very successful, but they weren't great movies. However it never would have happened. Eric wasn't a comic actor. His humour worked off the response of a live audience.' At heart, Eric was a front of curtain man – yet for once, his comic instincts let him down.

'I couldn't see the logic of moving from the BBC to ITV,' says Eddie Braben. 'We had a show that was high in the ratings and the best production team you could possibly have.' Braben had no interest in making movies, and he didn't rate Eric and Ernie's chances of big screen success. 'I never thought films would work for Morecambe & Wise,' he says. 'Once they came off the small, cosy living room screen, some of the magic was lost.' However Ernie's mind was made up, and for once, so was Eric's. 'He still wanted to kid himself that there was that big movie to be made,' says Gary. 'They'd have taken even less money to be at Thames, just to make that movie.'

In the meantime there were new TV shows to make for their new employer, but although Thames had bought up Eric and Ernie, they hadn't bought up their backroom boys. Their producer, Ernest Maxin, opted to stay at the BBC, and so (for the time

Eric leaving Harefield Hospital after his heart bypass operation in 1979.

being) did Eddie Braben. It was like hiring Michael Schumacher without Ferrari. Thames did the best they could, recruiting Barry Cryer and John Junkin, two of the best writers in the business, but it wasn't quite the same. Cryer and Junkin knew Eric and Ernie pretty well, having worked as their warm up men at the BBC, but only Eddie Braben really knew their sense of humour inside out.

Thames did their best to recreate the magic of the BBC shows, but trying to reproduce a classic is always a thankless task, and the difference between Eric and Ernie's last Christmas show for the BBC and their first one on ITV could scarcely have been more striking. The show's main talking point was a cameo by the recently retired Prime Minister, Harold Wilson, but news of his participation had been leaked the papers, and his muted, somewhat sheepish turn felt like an awkward anti-climax. Rising Damp star Leonard Rossiter also put in an appearance, but his wisecracking made Eric and Ernie look like two straight men. Morecambe & Wise were best at bouncing off classical actors, not comedians (or politicians). They were still several streets ahead of any other comics on the box, but after their record breaking finale for the BBC, it was a distinct disappointment.

The public voted with their feet. The viewing figure was a little over nineteen million – still a massive rating for any show, but nearly ten million down on the previous year's total. It was their first professional setback in a decade, but it was dwarfed by the personal setback that soon followed. In January 1979, Eric collapsed in the kitchen of his family home in Harpenden. 'I'll be all right in a minute,'[3] he told his son, Gary, but he wasn't. He'd had another heart attack. Gary called the doctor and Eric was rushed to hospital. 'The doctor told me afterwards it was touch and go,' remembers Gary. Thankfully, Eric survived, but pioneering heart surgeon Magdi Yacoub recommended that he have a triple bypass. 'What would happen if I didn't?' asked Eric. 'I wouldn't expect you to live more than a few months,' replied Yacoub. 'What are you doing this afternoon?' asked Eric.[4]

Bypass surgery was still science fiction when Eric had his first heart attack, and even in the hands of such an eminent surgeon it was bound to be a risky business. 'Mr Yacoub wasn't exactly encouraging,' said Eric. 'He said something about not listening to any long playing records or starting any serials.'[5] Mercifully, the seven hour operation was a success. 'It was like going through the first heart attack again but without any of the novelty factor,' says Gary. 'There's only so many times you can go on Parkinson and make a joke about it. When you're ten years older and it's the same again, it's not so funny.' However nobody remembered to tell Eric. When he came round, he was full of wisecracks, just like he had been first time around. 'They had no trouble putting me out before they operated,' he quipped. 'They showed me the bill. I went out like a light.'

Even as he left the hospital, the laughter didn't cease. Most people simply would have said, 'No comment,' but even in such dire straits, Eric still felt duty bound to raise a laugh. 'What was the hospital cocoa like?' asked one of the small army of reporters waiting on the steps outside. 'Marvellous stuff,' said Eric. 'It's green.' 'You've obviously got to take it easy for a bit?' enquired another. 'Well, if I can get a bit, I'll take it, easy,' said Eric. He wasn't allowed too much excitement, he said – but he was still allowed to kiss the wife. His compulsion to keep the public entertained was paramount, and the press would happily have kept him there all day, if they'd had their way. 'Intensive care unit, please,' he said, climbing into his waiting car. As they drove away at last, beyond the gaze of the TV cameras, he sank back into the seat, and turned to Joan. 'Didn't do

Keep Britain Tidy.

too bad, did I love?'[6] he said, but he couldn't fool his wife. Eric's funny bone was still in perfect shape, but Joan could tell his heart was no longer in it. This time, for the first time, he would have loved to have sneaked out the back way.

Back home in Harpenden, Eric was determined to take it easy, though his idea of clean living wasn't quite what the doctor ordered. 'No Smoking or Drinking Before 7pm' read the notice he put up in his living room – not much of a curfew for a man recovering from a second heart attack. 'My limit is one large scotch and two ounces of tobacco a day,' he said. 'I'm not going to give up my pipe because I really enjoy it, but I'm cutting down hard on the booze. I know I was drinking too much. Half a bottle of wine with my lunch, then maybe five large scotches during the evening, and chain smoking cigars at the same time. It just did not make sense for a man with a history of heart trouble.'[7] It hardly made sense for a man with a completely clean bill of health, but it was an improvement nonetheless. He loosened his ties with Luton Town FC, stepping down from director to vice president ('I get all the facilities,' he explained, 'and no aggravation when we lose') and focused on bird watching instead of golf. Now

Jimmy Saville fixes it for Eric to smoke one of his Havana cigars. At the time, Eric was busy negotiating a deal with a tobacco company, whereby they would give him free cigars in exchange for photo opportunities at public events. This arrangement was abruptly shelved following his second heart attack.

that Gail and Gary were grown up, Eric and Joan had adopted another son, Steven, who shared Eric's love of fishing. A tranquil retirement lay ahead of him, if only his health would last. All his favourite pastimes were solitary, (it was the only way he could stop himself from being the life and soul of the party) but fishing was his greatest love. It didn't even matter if he didn't catch anything. 'He'd sit on the riverbank all day,' says Gary. 'It was just the pleasure of being there that was a great escape for him. On the golf course, or at a charity cricket match, he had to be Eric Morecambe, but on the riverbank, he could just be himself.'

Although he couldn't bear to give up his pipe, Eric took a complete break from television. He took the rest of the year off from Thames, but even now, he couldn't bear to remain idle for long. Instead of putting his feet up, he finished his first novel, Mr Lonely. At first he mainly did it out of boredom, to fill the listless days he spent convalescing, but as the writing gathered pace, his enthusiasm grew. 'For a long while he had held himself back because he thought book writing could only be done by people who'd had a good education,' recalls Joan. 'To his astonishment, he found it

Lords Taverners charity cricket match. Left to right: **actor Roy Kinnear, Eric, newsreader Reginald Bosanquet.**

Eric doing what he liked to do best.

remarkably easy.'[8] It was an extremely accomplished debut, but what was most surprising was its dark tone. It was set in the familiar world of show business, but apart from a few friendly in jokes about friends and colleagues, it was a million miles away from Eric's amiable public image. Its hero (or anti hero) is a thoroughly unpleasant (and thoroughly unfunny) stand up comic called Sid Lewis, who somehow makes the break from club compere to TV superstar. Sid is dishonest, mean spirited and adulterous – the complete opposite of Eric, in fact. The first half of the book is a sort of nightmare vision of what might have become of Eric if he'd never hit the big time. The second half is a kind of cautionary tale about what the big time could have done to him if he hadn't been such a decent chap. Despite the considerable handicap of a completely unsympathetic central character, the book was well received, though anyone who only knew Eric from Morecambe & Wise would have been surprised (if not shocked) by its misanthropic content.

Eric was modest about his new career, insisting he never would have made it into print if he hadn't been famous. 'I'm not an author – I'm only a writer,' he said. Yet his subsequent children's books, The Reluctant Vampire and The Vampire's Revenge, were both published in translation on the Continent, where Morecambe & Wise were virtually unknown, indicating that whatever got him into print in the first place, he

753 FJH

remained in print on merit. These jolly romps, about a friendly vampire who sups nothing stronger than blood orange juice, were much closer to Eric's affable screen persona. For a lad who'd left school at fifteen, with no qualifications whatsoever, writing thrilled him in a way that performing never could. 'If Sadie had had an education, she'd have made a great writer,' says Joan, and given a bit more time to hone his work, Eric would have made a very good one. Flattered by the highbrow acclaim, he resolved to write a book a year – but in the meantime, there was the small matter of a TV series to attend to.

'I know it's easy with hindsight, but I do look back and shake my head and think, "Why did he even bother?" says Gary. 'Just forget the film, and come to an agreement with Thames. Give up the contract, just get out of it – even if it costs a few hundred grand.' But for all his success, Eric was still a child of the Depression. His was a generation of hard graft and obligation. Such a decision would have been utterly alien to his nature. 'He never liked letting anyone down – not as Eric Morecambe. He could let us all down as a father, and let my mother down as a husband, but he couldn't let anyone down as Eric Morecambe. He was always so protective of that.'

There was one body of opinion that could have persuaded him to stop, and that was the medical profession. But that ultimatum never came. 'I remember doctors and even the surgeons saying, "Well, he shouldn't really do it, but we didn't want to tell him that because we knew that he couldn't have stopped,"' says Gary, 'but if someone had said to him, "This will kill you," he would have stopped that day. Yet no one ever said that. It was a massive misunderstanding because they were looking at the Eric of ten years earlier, when he was in his forties. He probably couldn't have stopped at that time, but he was a very different guy by 1980. He appreciated that things were slowing down, that Morecambe & Wise were in their twilight years. He enjoyed his time at home much more. He had learned to relax and do more peaceful things. If someone had said, "Don't ever work again," he would have said, "Fine." But no one ever said that to him. He was never good at making his own decisions. I think he wanted to pass the responsibility to someone else.' But this was a decision only Eric could make, and ultimately, it was a decision he was incapable of making. Just four months after his heart bypass, Eric returned to the studio. 'I feel uncomfortable even talking about it,' says Gary. 'I just think, "What on earth was he doing?'

John Ammonds and Eddie Braben were both enticed back to the programme, and with the old team back together again, the shows started to pick up. Their 1980 series topped the ratings, but Eric was bored, and even Ammonds felt the spark had gone.

'There was a shortage of material,' says Gary. 'They were regurgitating a lot of stuff they'd done twenty years earlier.' And even the new stuff wasn't quite the same. 'They were desperate for material by then,' says Joan, 'and Eddie was getting so run down.' Eddie Braben's biggest bugbear was the adverts. 'You were used to seeing Morecambe & Wise for fifty minutes non-stop on the BBC, and then you watch them on ITV for eight minutes and they're snatched away,' says Braben. 'It's broken in the middle and it's hard to pick up again after that.'

Ernie still dreamt of Hollywood, but for Eric the showbiz dream had lost its lustre. He'd always been a lovely mover (a talent he'd inherited from his father) but now he found dancing difficult. Strangely, the surgery had even affected his immaculate comic timing. John Ammonds found he had to edit their routines – something he'd never done before.

Far worse was to follow. While filming a Keystone Cops pastiche, Eric ran into a wall and knocked his heart out of rhythm. He was bundled off to hospital, where he spent a couple of nights recuperating. 'I won't be here this time next year,' he told Joan. 'Don't be silly,' she said.[9] Comedy is a kind of Midas touch, and it was Eric's curse that even when he was in deadly earnest, even those who were closest too him found it hard to take him seriously. 'He told a neighbour that he wouldn't be around next year,' says Gary. 'She thought he was just messing around.'

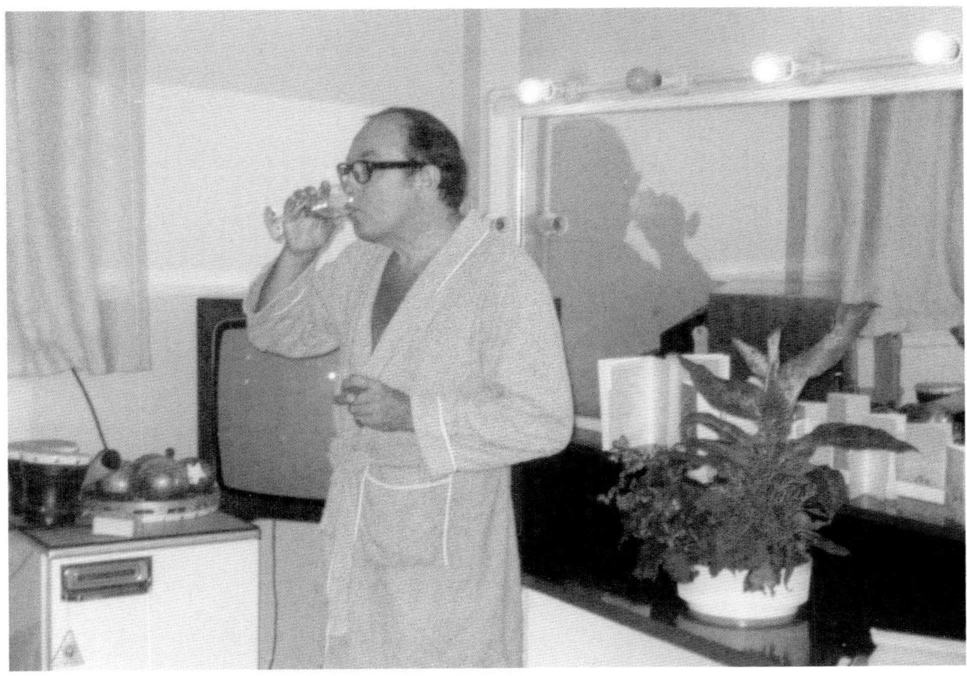

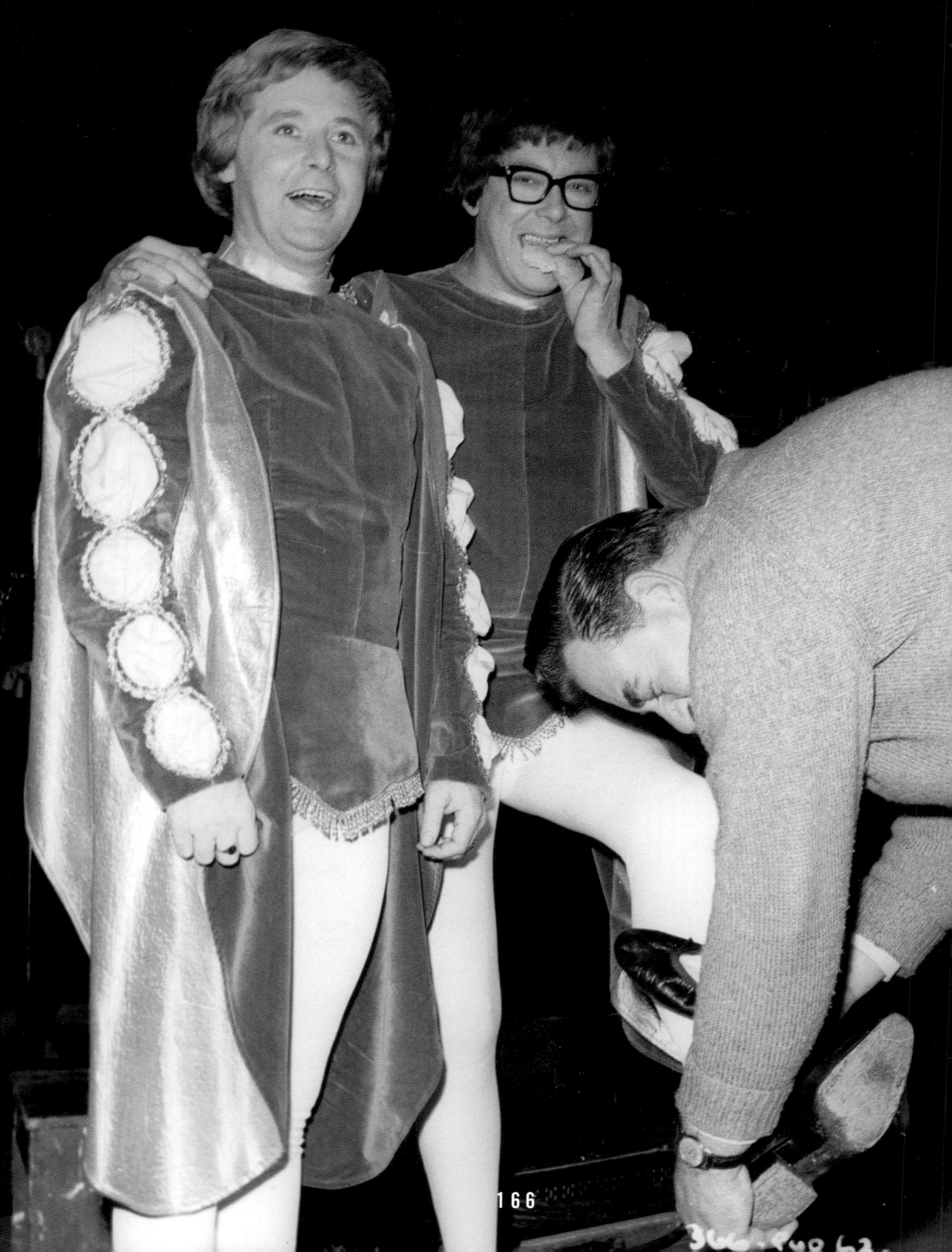

Despite Eric's gloomy prognosis, it seemed no lasting damage had been done, but his confidence had suffered yet another knock. 'I'm not enjoying this anymore,' he told Ernie. 'I've had enough. I think I ought to stop it. What do you think I should do?'[10] He said the same thing to Gary. Both of them replied that only Eric could decide. Yet Eric hated making decisions. Much as he wanted to, he found it impossible to break free. He set off for a lunch with Thames, determined to take a year off rather than sign another contract, only to return home having signed up for three more years.

'Why do you continue doing it?' asked his friend, Dickie Davies. 'I'm not sure I've got enough,' said Eric. 'Enough money?' asked Davies, incredulously. 'You've got a Rolls Royce, you've got a chauffeur, you've got a lovely home. More important, you've got a beautiful wife and you've got the family around you. What more do you need?' 'Yes, but as you get older you need a bit more money,'[11] replied Eric. You could take the boy out of the Northern town, but you couldn't take the Northern town out of the boy. Even after all these years, a great deal of fame and no small fortune, he hadn't forgotten his grandfather's advice – that real freedom is in your wallet.

Sir John Mills plots his great escape. Sir John said that working with Eric & Ernie was one of the greatest moments of his career.

For Eric, Night Train To Murder was a bitter disappointment. 'I think that did break Eric's heart,' says his wife, Joan. 'He couldn't believe that anything could be so bad.' Sadly, this film, intended for the big screen but only ever transmitted on television, was the last thing he did with Ernie.

'The only accurate barometer of success in show business is the money you make,'[12] said Eric, but there was another reason why he carried on, even when his heart could take no more, and that was his loyalty to Ernie. Ernie had never had a day's illness in his life. He was in no hurry to retire. He'd passed up the prospect of becoming the British Mickey Rooney for a selfless career as Eric's straight man, and after forty years of faithful service, Eric felt it would be unfair to simply walk away. 'He was still on the treadmill,' says Gary, sadly, 'and he was on it until the day he died.'

The pressure of performing was killing him, but there was a part of him that thrived on it, and the same went for the recognition that went with it. 'Unlike a lot of entertainers, he knew you can't beat the press,' says Gary. 'He loved the fact that they'd ring, even during Sunday lunch, because that meant they were still interested in him. That feeds the ego. It feeds the machine. He used to go to inordinate lengths to disguise himself when he went to Harpenden. He'd wear a coat and a hat, walk with a limp and take off his glasses. He'd still usually get recognised, but if he didn't he'd be really upset. Then he'd do something to get recognised, and defeat the whole object of it. He used to say to me that he got fed up with people asking him for autographs, but he would have been much more fed up if they'd stopped.'

The TV shows trundled on, and even though Eric was feeling the strain, he never lost the ability to laugh at his parlous state of health. 'Any more like that,' he'd quip, after a star guest had done a turn, 'and I'll have to go back on the tablets.' But it wasn't just the tablets he had to worry about. By now, he'd been fitted with a pacemaker. 'Do they ever go wrong?' asked Max Bygraves. 'It went wrong this morning,' said Eric. 'What happened?' asked Bygraves. 'I farted,' said Eric, 'and the garage doors opened.'[13]

In 1983 Eric and Ernie embarked on their long awaited movie for Thames' film subsidiary, Euston Films – supposedly the reason they'd left the BBC in the first place. However Euston Films barely bore comparison with the Rank Organisation, let alone any of the American studios that Ernie still pined for. It had been set up to make the first British TV movies, and though it did that job very well, it was hardly Pinewood, let alone Hollywood.[14]

Eric and Ernie's movie, Night Train To Murder, didn't sound too bad on paper – a creepy comic caper that harked back to the Saturday morning movies of their youth – but the result was something else. 'It was dreadful,' says Joan. 'I think that did break Eric's heart. He was given the video to watch and he sat hypnotised. He couldn't believe what he was watching. He couldn't believe that anything could be so bad. He wanted it buried, which you can't do. They'd spent a lot of money on it. But he could not believe that they could have got it so wrong.' It was hard to believe they'd left the BBC, and Ernest Maxin, and Eddie Braben, for this. Eric was so unhappy with the movie, he wanted Thames to screen it during children's hour – or ideally in the middle of the night. Mercifully, transmission was postponed, for the time being, but it confirmed Eric's hunch that his lifelong partnership with Ernie had finally reached its natural end.

Below. Left to Right: **Eric, Roy Castle, Ernie. Eric introduced Roy to his wife, Fiona. Roy told Eric that he fancied Fiona and was dying to meet her, so Eric took Fiona to Roy's dressing room, said, 'Fiona, I'd like you to meet my friend Roy, he's desperately in love with you,' and walked out, leaving the two of them alone together, tongue-tied and red-faced. Roy and Fiona were blissfully happy together, but Roy still used to joke that if they ever had a row, he'd feel like throwing stones at Eric's windows.**

Right: **Eric with TV presenter Selina Scott.**

Above: **Eric & Ernie play reindeer to Bruce Forsyth's Santa.**

Below: **When will I see you again? Eric & Ernie, The Three Degrees and The Crankies.**

Game for a laugh. Left to Right: **Henry Kelly, Matthew Kelly, Eric, Sarah Kennedy, Jeremy Beadle.**

Left to right, **actor John Alderton, actress Beryl Reid and Eric, on location in Norfolk, filming a series for Anglia TV, based on the poems of poet laureate Sir John Betjeman.**

Chapter 10

Bring Me Sunshine

'Bring me sunshine in your smile, bring me laughter all the while...'

'If I have another heart attack, it'll kill me,' Eric told Joan, 'and if I do another Morecambe & Wise series, I'll have another heart attack.'[1] There was nothing hysterical about this prediction. Countless comics had died of heart failure, from Sid James to Peter Sellers, many of them in the course of their uniquely stressful work. 'What happened to dear old Sid must stand as a warning to me,' said Eric, turning down a plea to perform a fundraising gig to save Morecambe's Winter Gardens, where his mum and dad first met. 'Sid had one coronary, but went on working just as hard – and then died onstage. I couldn't let the same thing happen to me.'[2] In 1984, yet another showbiz pal, Tommy Cooper, died in exactly the same way. Eric's mind was made up. Whatever else he did, there would be no more Morecambe & Wise. 'I'm tired of being funny,'[3] he told Gary, but mainly he was just tired.

If anything, Eric would have liked to have retired even earlier. He'd always said that comics peak between thirty and fifty, and Eric and Ernie were now in their late fifties, with more than forty miles on the showbiz clock. 'They actually looked like older men,' says Gary. 'Ernie's hair had gone white and Eric was getting very jowly.' Eric didn't want to pack it in completely, but the remorseless slog of a weekly TV series no longer held any allure. 'We've been at the top of the Light Entertainment tree since 1963,' he told Gary. 'When we first started, we weren't sure if we'd even be able to run to a second series.'[4] He'd been planning his retirement for years, and now the finishing line was finally in sight. 'Anything after sixty five is a bonus, career wise,' he said, 'and most important, you can travel on the buses free.'[5]

There was no danger of becoming bored. He had his hobbies and his writing and his after dinner speaking – a breeze after all his years on TV and in the halls. 'I've got to the stage, after two or three heart attacks, where it doesn't worry me anymore,' he'd tell his fellow diners. 'If you don't laugh, you don't leave – it's as simple as that.' Doing theatre shows had become a tougher prospect, but there was one way he could go onstage without putting too much strain on his heart. For a while, he'd been toying with the idea of doing theatrical question and answer sessions, and now he received an invitation which would allow him to try out this new idea. He'd been invited to do a sit down interview in front of a live audience at the Roses Theatre in Tewkesbury. It was the perfect place to test drive his plan. The Roses was a small provincial venue, away from the spotlight, and the request came from Stan Stennett, an old friend and colleague from his Variety days.

Eric was looking forward seeing Stan, but his health remained a worry. He'd been suffering from chest pains, and he looked drawn and grey. A few days before the show, he went to see the doctor. 'Joan and I have come for some advice about family planning,'[6] he said, but the diagnosis was no joke. He had an enlarged heart, and needed

to return to hospital for more tests. 'We'd had a dreadful week,' says Joan. 'His health was touch and go and it was a terrible dilemma. We had the cardiac chap in the night before, doing another test on him. What do we do? Do we let Stan down?'

They had half a mind to cancel, but Stan had sold a lot of tickets, and Eric didn't want to disappoint an old friend. 'Don't you feel this would be stressful for you, that you shouldn't take this chance?' asked Joan. 'Oh, no, love,' said Eric. 'I'll really enjoy it. It'll be good fun.' 'But it'll still be stressful,' said Joan. 'Without the adrenalin, you can't perform.' 'Oh, no,' said Eric. 'We'll make it a fun weekend.' 'In hindsight I wish I'd been more forceful,' she says. 'If I'd been more domineering, he'd never have done the damn show.' But there was really no way she could have stopped him, and so the next day, six weeks after Tommy Cooper's death, Eric set off for Tewkesbury, with Joan, as ever, by his side. Despite his dodgy ticker, he was in high spirits. Joan checked into the hotel, and found he'd booked the bridal suite, complete with four poster bed. 'You've waited a long time for a honeymoon, but at last you're having one!'[7] said Eric. 'We arranged for the chef to stay on and do us all a meal,' says Joan. 'It was going to be Eric's treat.'

Eric in mañana mood.

The theatre was packed. Eric came on to a standing ovation, and the show went like a dream. It's a shame no one thought to record it. Eric talked about all sorts of things, things he hadn't talked about in years, things he'd never talked about at all, not even to Joan – from his wartime stint down the mines to Tommy Cooper and Diana Dors, two old friends who'd died that year. 'I don't want to die in front of an audience,'[8] he said, but for everyone else in the theatre, swept away on this flood of memories, dying was the last thing on anybody's mind. 'It was fascinating,' says Joan. 'The audience was absolutely spellbound. He was coming out with things that we knew nothing about.' Yet alone in this sea of strangers, Joan was becoming increasingly concerned. As the show wore on, Eric's voice was growing hoarser, and he was drinking more and more water in a futile attempt to clear his throat. Everyone else was engrossed, in no hurry to see him go. Only Joan could tell he was dying to get offstage. 'I'm sitting there in the audience, sweating,' she recalls. 'I knew that he was desperate to get off, and I was desperate for him.'

At last, the show ended, and Eric went off to Bring Me Sunshine, yet there was so much applause that he simply had to come back on and take another bow. He started horsing around with the band, playing the xylophone, sticks flying into the front stalls. 'In a very short time, the act had gone from a calm chat show to a slice of pure music hall,'[9] recalls Joan. 'I knew that he had to get off that stage. I could sense it. Nobody else could.'[10]

Finally, after six curtain calls, Eric took his last bow. 'That's your lot,' he said, and walked offstage. 'Thank God that's over,' he muttered, as he reached the sanctuary of the wings, and keeled over, hitting his head on the floor. Out front, the audience were still clapping when the cry went up, 'Is there a doctor in the house?' Joan knew it had to be her Eric. She dashed backstage, where she found a doctor giving her husband the kiss of life. The theatre went completely still, and the audience filed out in absolutely silence. 'It was as if everyone suddenly became mute,'[11] says Stan Stennett. It was as if they knew something dreadful was about to happen.

Eric was bundled into an ambulance, but although the doctor had got him breathing again, he was still unconscious. 'Talk to him!' the nurse told Joan, as they hurtled towards the nearest hospital. 'Try and get him out of it!'[12] Joan felt she ought to let him rest, but she did as she was told. 'Eric!' she said. 'Eric! Squeeze my hand if you can hear me!'[13] Eric didn't open his eyes, but he squeezed her hand tightly. 'Thank God!' thought Joan. 'He's going to make it!'[14] Yet though he reached the hospital alive, he never came round. Eric Morecambe died at 4am on Monday 28 May, 1984. He was 58 years old. 'His heart was just too weak,' the doctor told Joan. 'He couldn't take any more.'[15] 'I

Eric upstaged, for once in his life, by the late, great Tommy Cooper.

always knew that was going to be the end,' says Joan. 'I almost wish he hadn't gripped my hand so hard because then you knew he was fighting to come out of it.'[16] The bridal suite remained unslept in. They never did have a honeymoon. 'It was a fitting way for him to go, and he didn't die onstage, which he said he would have hated,' said Gary. A true pro to the very end, Eric made sure he finished the show. 'Comics don't live as long as straight men,'[17] said Ernie, and now Eric had proved him right.

Joan phoned Ernie in the early hours, and told him the news. An hour later, he drove to TVAM to do an interview he'd arranged weeks before. 'I thought twice before going,' he said, 'but in the end it seemed the right thing to do.'[18] He paid tribute to the man who'd been his other half for 43 years. 'It's the saddest day of my life,' he said. 'I feel like I've lost a limb.'[19] When Eric was recovering from his second heart attack, weary of constant enquiries about his partner's health, Ernie had taken to wearing a badge that read, 'Eric's much better, thank you, but I'm not feeling very well.' Today it was a badge that could have been worn by virtually everyone in the nation.

Eric's last Christmas, 1983.

A week later, on Monday 4 June, Eric was laid to rest at St Nicholas's in Harpenden. Silent crowds lined the route to the funeral. There were over a thousand uninvited mourners outside the church alone. Veteran comedian Dickie Henderson delivered the main address. He'd performed the same function at Arthur Askey's memorial service the year before, and Eric had been so impressed, he'd asked him to do his send off too. 'I would like to be cremated and my favourite music is Smoke Gets In Your Eyes,' he wrote to Dickie. 'I'll pay you when I see you down there. Nothing in this letter constitutes a contract.' Henderson didn't let him down. 'Whenever you think of Eric, you smile,' he said, 'and the entire nation feels that way.'[20]

Eric had told Joan, 'I don't want there to be any long faces,'[21] but Ernie moved the congregation to tears by reciting the lyrics to Bring Me Sunshine. It was more moving than anything he could have said. 'Goodbye Sunshine,' read the message on his wreath. 'Miss you, your little fat friend.' When Joan went back to the church, and looked in the remembrance book, she found that someone had drawn a pair of glasses beside her husband's name.

'Does that mean there won't be any more magic?'[22] asked Eric's three year old grandson, when he was told his granddad was dead. He meant the magic tricks Eric performed for him, but the rest of us were missing the magic he made with Ernie. The Telegraph called him a master comic, The Times called him a genius, but perhaps the most fitting eulogy came from Nancy Banks-Smith in The Guardian. 'A TV set is not a bad box to be buried in when you have been the best on the box,'[23] she wrote, harking back to the clipping that Eric carried around in his wallet for thirty years. 'I don't know what I'm doing here,' said Des O'Connor, at Eric's tribute show at the London Palladium. 'They're all saying nice things about Eric. He never said anything nice about me.'[24] It was one of the funniest jokes he'd ever cracked. Eric would have enjoyed it immensely. 'There's only one Eric Morecambe,' sang the crowd at Luton Town's next home game. He would have enjoyed that even more. 'That was very moving,' says Gary, whose happiest memory of his father was sitting alongside him in the main stand at Luton games.

A few years after Eric died, Luton actually got to Wembley, to play Arsenal in the League Cup final, and Gary and his brother Steven went along. It was an amazing game. Arsenal were hot favourites, and for the first eighty minutes, the match ran true to form. With ten minutes to play, Arsenal were winning two one. The only real surprise was that they weren't winning by three or four. They'd hit the post. They'd hit the bar. They'd even missed a penalty. Yet somehow Luton clung on, and clawed their way back to win three two. 'I was very tearful afterwards,' says Gary. 'Dad would have been so proud. He missed their finest hour. A Wembley final! Can you imagine? It was a real tearjerker for us at the end. It was a beautiful sunny day, as well.'

Eric and Gary at Morecambe Football Club.

Eric turns out for England, alongside fellow striker Kevin Keegan.

Below: **You can't see the join.**

MORECAMBE & WISE

c **Morecambe didn't** live a long time, but he lived through a time of ıendous change. He started off in Variety and ended up on television, and more any other comedian, he made this medium his own. Only a handful of music hall ics made the transition from the big stage to the small screen, and the only one achieved anything like the same success was Ernie. So why did Eric and Ernie eed where so many other comics failed?

A lot of it was due to the unique chemistry between them, but it was a chemistry was refined over an extraordinary span of years. As Graham McCann points out, is absorbing biography, Laurel & Hardy were already in their thirties when they ıme a double act – Eric and Ernie were still in their teens. Eric and Ernie grew up ther, but onstage they remained the age they were when they first met. 'The acters they present in their act are both fixed at a mental and emotional age of oximately fifteen,' wrote Kenneth Tynan. 'Such is their sexual innocence that ough they frequently share a bed in TV sketches, no whiff of queerness ever udes.'[1] 'There was never a dirty joke, never a four letter word,' observes Eddie en. 'Bloody, Bugger and Sod It – that was as bad as it ever got.'[2]

Eric and Ernie never swore. You almost felt they wouldn't know how to. But that was only a small part of their appeal. Above all, they reminded us of the Britain they grew up in, a Britain the rest of us had somehow lost along the way. 'People liked the fact that they were two men who were happily married,' says Joan, astutely. Even the normally waspish Kenneth Williams praised their 'honesty and goodness'[3], a quality which he sensed, quite rightly, accounted for their universal appeal. Fame corrupts and absolute fame corrupts absolutely, but Eric and Ernie's showbiz ascent was so gradual that they were never spoiled by overnight success. 'We always had to fight to prove we were good, from the beginning to the end,'[4] said Eric, and that eternal struggle kept them humble,

even when they were household names. They never lorded it over anyone, least of all the paying public. Unlike a lot of stars, they even took newspaper inaccuracies in their stride. 'Go and get the papers,' Eric would tell Ernie. 'See if we've split up again.'

Joan said Eric and Ernie were closer than husband and wife. Like many a married couple, they even finished each other's sentences. Yet while a lot of other double acts ended in divorce, Eric and Ernie sustained their partnership by restricting their relationship to office hours. They stayed in separate hotels on tour and rarely saw each other socially. During the last fifteen years of Eric's life, Ernie only visited him at home three times. 'They were very independent,' says Gary. 'I can't remember one time I saw Ernie at the house. I went to his house once, but that was after my father died.'

From the late Fifties to the early Eighties, no other double act could touch them. Peter Cook and Dudley Moore were the only comic duo to match them, but even Pete and Dud never enjoyed such incredibly broad appeal. Eric was never remotely worried by the competition, quite simply because there wasn't any. Someone once asked him what they would have been if they hadn't become comedians. 'Mike and Bernie Winters,'[5] he replied.

Eric and Ernie do an interview for BBC Radio. 'What would you have been if you hadn't become comedians?' the presenter asked them. 'Mike and Bernie Winters,' quipped Eric.

'There were two old men sitting in deckchairs...'

During the late Eighties and early Nineties, their childlike comedy fell out of fashion. The class conflict of the Thatcher years inspired an angry, hectoring style of humour that became known as Alternative Comedy. For a few years, stand up comics talking politics was all that seemed to matter, and Eric and Ernie's gentle act briefly became old hat. However audiences soon grow tired of being shouted at, and as Margaret Thatcher made way for John Major, and subsequently Tony Blair, confrontational comics like Alexei Sayle made way for clowns like Vic Reeves and Harry Hill – both of whom bore more than a passing resemblance to the late, great Eric Morecambe.

Normally, nothing dates like dead comedians, yet as Eric's death receded into memory, the more we missed his boyish banter, and the more we realised an act like theirs wouldn't come around again. 'The double acts of today don't have the same warmth as Morecambe & Wise,' says Penelope Keith, a guest on their record breaking Christmas Show. 'Fry & Laurie and French & Saunders are laughed at by the chattering classes, but they don't span the range of Morecambe & Wise.'[6] 'Broad is usually the term for bawdy, basic humour, which theirs certainly wasn't, but they had broad appeal,' concurs Rowan Atkinson, who met Eric early on in his career. 'It's difficult to find that these days – something which all the family, from the age of six to sixty, can enjoy.'[7] And although it took them a while to come around to the idea, the BBC agreed. In 1994, they marked the tenth anniversary of Eric's death with a compilation show fronted by Ben Elton, a lifelong Morecambe & Wise fan. 'They remind me of Vladimir and Estragon in Beckett's Waiting For Godot,' observed Elton, 'filling in time, looking back on the past.'[8] The general public was just as enthusiastic. Bring Me Sunshine was bettered only by EastEnders in the BBC's ratings, and a repeat of their 1971 Christmas show attracted a similarly enthusiastic response.

The same year, back in Morecambe, Eric's old local paper, The Visitor, began a campaign to erect a statue of Eric in the town that gave him his name. Five years later, it was finally unveiled, amid much pomp and ceremony, not by some local civic dignitary, but (at her own personal request) by Her Majesty the Queen. 'You see statues to people on horseback with swords or rifles, people who killed people,' said Eddie Braben, as he watched Her Majesty do the honours, on the seafront where Eric used to go fishing with his father as a lad. 'Here's one being unveiled of a man who made people laugh.'[9] 'He was a genius,' declared Robin Day, who was also at the ceremony. 'I was on the show several times, notably when I was hit over the head with a bottle. I wouldn't have missed it for the world.'[10]

There was one guest of honour who was conspicuous by his absence. Ernie had died two months before, following a triple heart bypass, at the age of 73. 'We have had ups and downs for quite a while,' said his wife, Doreen, 'but he is finally gone.'[11] Thanks to Doreen, and his many friends, the fifteen years since Eric's death had been personally fulfilling, but professionally it was never going to be an easy time. He kept busy, touring Australia with a one man show and appearing in West End shows like Ray Cooney's Run For Your Wife, but there remained a cold draught down one side of him where Eric used to be. In 1990, he published his autobiography. Poignantly, it was entitled Still On My Way To Hollywood. It was dedicated to Eric, 'the best partner a man could have.' Yet when the BBC made Bring Me Sunshine, Ernie wasn't even interviewed. 'We didn't want too many talking heads,'[12] they said. Ernie was disappointed, but he shouldn't have been too surprised. Being a straight man has always been a thankless task.

Ernie kept in good shape, jogging into his sixties, but the strain of a lifetime in the spotlight began to tell. He suffered a stroke in 1993, and another one in 1995. On his seventieth birthday, after more than sixty years in show business, he announced his

retirement, though he'd really retired the day that Eric died. Ernie said the title of his autobiography would become his epitaph. 'I'm still on my way,' he'd say, long after his Hollywood hopes had faded. In the end, the closest he came was a holiday home in Florida. 'I always imagined I'd be another Mickey Rooney,' said Ernie, in a joint interview with Eric, just a few years before Eric died. 'You became Ernie Wise,' said Eric. 'Isn't that enough?' 'It's what dreams are made of,' said Ernie. 'We made that dream,' said Eric. 'The dream came true. It's here.'[13]

'Ernie still had his little dream about Hollywood, which always amused me, because Hollywood isn't the same,' says Joan. 'It's all finished, that era. It's all over.' The Hollywood Ernie dreamt about was the Hollywood of his youth, not the Hollywood of his autumn years. The difference between Eric and Ernie was that Eric knew the difference. It's a crying shame that they never made a British version of The Odd Couple, but it's hard to imagine them in any Hollywood movie of the last thirty years.

Ernie used to call himself the nation's cheerer-upper, and before he died, he gave his blessing to a venture that would continue this job from beyond the grave. For several years, Eric's son Gary had been trying to get a Morecambe & Wise stage show off the ground, but the question of who would play the leading roles had always defeated him. This problem was finally solved when theatre producer David Pugh handed over this project to a duo called the Right Size, aka Sean Foley and Hamish McColl.

Foley and McColl trained as actors, but they also write their own plays, and their knockabout performance style owes a lot to clowning and music hall. A few years before, they'd written and performed a tragicomic slapstick show called Stop Calling Me Vernon, about a vaudeville duo on the slide, and their Morecambe & Wise tribute was written and performed in much the same style. Rather than trying to impersonate Eric and Ernie, Foley and McColl wrote a play about a far less successful double act, hired by David Pugh to put on a show about Morecambe & Wise. It's a fascinating snapshot of the act that Eric and Ernie might have been if they'd never hit the big time, but although the similarities were uncanny, the result went way beyond simple mimicry. 'It's a sideways tribute,' says Gary, 'and that's what Eric would have liked.' Eddie Braben joined the writing team, Gary lent a hand, and The Play What I Wrote became a hit in London's West End, and in New York too. Eric and Ernie had made it in America, at long last. 'If Eric had been told, "In thirty years there's going to be a play about your life on Broadway," he never would have believed it,' says Gary. And nor would we.

There were a few dissenting voices. 'This isn't Eric and Ernie!' complained a

disgruntled fan. 'We should demand our bloody money back!'[14] Yet almost everyone else recognised that this oblique homage was far more fitting than some superficial impersonation. And it conjured up the essence of their act far better than an impersonation ever could. 'God, they were great,' remembered Gary, when he saw the show on the opening night. He was not alone. 'They were loved,' says Joan. 'They really were loved.' The reason Eric and Ernie were adored was because their humour wasn't motivated by malice, but by affection. And that is why that adoration endures.

'I've been in theatres where I'll swear to god that audience would pick them up and cuddle them if they could,' says Eddie Braben. 'Superstars, really big stars, go out onto a stage and they get, "Ooh!" When Eric and Ernie walked out, it was "Aah!" Audiences felt that everything was as it should be when they saw Eric and Ernie. They felt comfortable and they felt at home and they felt that they were with two dear friends.' With The Play What I Wrote, Eric and Ernie's act had come full circle. 'We took music hall into the television studio,' says Braben, and although it was Hamish McColl and Sean Foley up onstage, it felt like Eric and Ernie had finally returned home.

Audiences adored The Play What I Wrote, and the critics loved it too. 'Both a joyous recreation of Morecambe & Wise and an acute study of the emotional and professional interdependence on which any double act relies,'[15] wrote Michael Billington in The Guardian. Like the all best entertainers, Eric had left his audience wanting more. The Play What I Wrote won an Olivier award for best new play, and best of all, celebs queued up to play the show's guest star, just as they had done on telly twenty years before. Ralph Fiennes did the honours on the first night, followed by (in no particular order) Kylie Minogue, Ewan McGregor, Charles Dance, Nigel Havers, David Suchet, Cilla Black, Dawn French, Sting and Richard E Grant. Roger Moore played the part more than forty times – Eric and Ernie had asked him to appear with them, but he'd always been too busy playing James Bond. Twenty years after Eric's death, The Play What I Wrote was still touring. Sadie would have been proud of him. Those dancing lessons had paid off, after all.

Eric with his mum, Sadie.

The Big Match. Jimmy Hill hears Eric's excuses for another Luton defeat. With Elton John, Eric and Jimmy formed the Goaldiggers, a charity which raised funds for the National Playing Fields Association. 'We played the odd football match,' recalled Jimmy, 'one at Windsor, with the Duke of Edinburgh (our coach) and Eric (our linesman) supporting us from the touchline.'

Eric fooling around backstage.

Opposite page: **Eric on holiday in Majorca, 1955.**

This page: **Gary, Eric and Joan outside their villa in Portugal.**

Above: **Lifelong companions. The strain of forty three years together begins to show as Eric & Ernie put on their make up for Night Train To Murder.**

Chapter 12

Unfinished Fiction

When he died, in 1984, we'd probably seen the best of Eric Morecambe the comedian, but Eric Morecambe the writer was still only just getting started. He'd written two enchanting children's books (about a friendly vampire) and a jolly tome about his favourite hobby, fishing. His first full length novel, Mr Lonely, had been a promising venture into adult fiction, and he was already hard at work on a second, which showed every sign of being even better. Like Mr Lonely, Stella was about the bleaker side of show business, but unlike Mr Lonely, it had a highly sympathetic central character – a feisty yet sensitive aspiring starlet called Stella Ravenscroft. Completed by Eric's son, Gary, Stella was published in 1986, two years after Eric's death – but although Gary did a good job, Stella remains a story of what might have been.

However Stella wasn't the only work of fiction that Eric left in his study. He'd also been working on a short story, which remained unread and undiscovered (even by Gary) until today. Tantalisingly it's also incomplete, but it's clear that Eric had not abandoned it. 'Try to finish' reads a handwritten note scrawled across the first page. After all these years, you can only wonder where Eric's muse would have taken him, but even in its unfinished form, it's an intriguing insight into a side of Eric that Morecambe & Wise fans never saw. The health concerns that Eric describes seem distinctly autobiographical, but the simmering tension between this husband and wife (a world away from Eric and Joan's happy marriage) displays the power of his imagination and his growing prowess as a writer.

'You must try and lose some of that weight.'

Madeline looked at her husband's stomach.

'Oh, I'm not too bad.'

Ralph looked down at ten pounds of extra him that wasn't there last Chistmas. In five months he had put on all this weight.

'Anyway, a couple of extra pounds is easy to get off. A grapefruit diet, or an egg diet, or a banana diet... The drinking man's diet, that's the one! I'll go on that!'

He looked pleased as he put the last spoonful of chocolate cake into his mouth, and sipped the glass of claret while he eyed the bottle of port on the sideboard.

'Is there any stilton left, darling?' he asked. 'And a couple of biscuits – not too many.'

He slapped what could only be described as a belly a couple of times and smiled.

'My god, maybe she's right,' he thought to himself, as he tapped the extra ten pounds.

He fastened the button of his jacket.

'You see, there's no problem. I can still fasten the old jacket.'

'New jacket.'

'Eh?'

'New jacket. That sports jacket is no more than six weeks old – and you were measured for it. If you were to let your stomach relax right now, that button could become a lethal weapon – and you would also become a normal colour.'

She picked up her serviette that had fallen on the floor. As she bent down, he relaxed his stomach – quickly. Madeline heard the button hit the bottle of port on the sideboard. She looked at him and slowly shook her head.

'Yes, the drinking man's diet – that's the one. I'm told you can lose a stone within ten or twelve days.'

'There will be no drinking man's diet in this house. I've just watched you this evening. Do you know how much you've had to drink since you came in from the office? Well, I'll tell you. You have been in this house one hour and a half, and in that time…'

'Charlie's on the drinking man's diet and he's lost…'

'… Two dry martinis, large – stirred not shaken, except when you go to the loo – a bottle of claret, you'll now go on the port and finish your meal with a brandy. And we've only had fish and chips.'

She picked the button off the sideboard and handed it to him.

'There you are, dear. Keep it as a souvenir. Put it in your top pocket as a keepsake, because I won't be sewing it back on.'

He took the button from her and kept it in his hand.

'If you had worn your waistcoat tonight I could be in the doctor's surgery now, having waistcoat buttons removed from my face.'

She left the dining room with a handful of plates.

'Coffee?' she asked, as she got to the door.

'Er, yes please, dear.'

'Black?' she asked, sarcastically.

But before he could answer, she left the room.

He sat in the dining room, looking at the button. He heard his wife rattling pots in the kitchen, and filling the kettle at the tap. He put the button down on the table. His hand went automatically to the stem of his half empty wine glass. He swirled the drink around the glass and brought it to his lips. The glass was three inches away from his lips when his brain told him not to have anymore. Unfortunately, his arm wasn't listening. His brain turned his head from the drink, but his arm tipped the glass. The wine went down his chin, onto the front of his white shirt. He heard the kettle whistle. Quickly, he wiped his chin with the back of his hand, grabbed the serviette, and tucked it into his collar to hide the stain.

Madeline came back into the room with his coffee on a tray and put it in front of him – just a single cup of black coffee, some brown sugar and a spoon. She didn't speak as she left him alone in the dining room. He sat there for a while, looking at the cup of coffee. He took a small sip and put the cup down.

He rose slowly. As he did so, the weight of his stomach dropped a matter of a few inches, forcing his flies down about the same distance. He took the port bottle and opened the sideboard, putting the bottle out of sight within the cupboard. As he pulled his arm from within the cupboard, there was no bottle of port in it. Like a magician, he had changed the port into a bottle of brandy. He drank half of the black coffee, then replenished the cup with brandy. He took out a Castella from his inside pocket, straightened it and lit it. As he smoked, he heard the TV, entertaining his wife with yet another rerun of Last of The Summer Wine.

He went to bed early that night, leaving his wife to lock up. When Madeline entered the bedroom, Ralph had been asleep a good hour. She looked at him, lying on his back, covered only by a white bed sheet. His stomach, under the tightened sheet, looked like a good location for The Sound of Music.

Chapter 13

THE DIARIES 1967

ERIC ONLY KEPT a diary for a few years, but he kept it during a pivotal period of his life. When he wrote the first entry, in 1967, he was still slogging away in summer season at Great Yarmouth. When he wrote the last entry, in 1969, he was back in Harpenden recovering from his first heart attack. It's intriguing to read what he was really thought about these events at the time, rather than the way he looked back on them with hindsight. A lot of Eric's observations are fairly matter of fact, but the more intimate entries cast fresh light on his work, while the descriptive passages read like a dry run for his future fiction. And although his private voice is a good deal graver and more reflective than his public persona, the same impish sense of fun remains.

This book was bought in Yarmouth, August 15 1967 – price 35 shillings, while playing summer season with Ernie Wise. Salary – £3000 per week between us. At that type of money I should have bought a bigger book.

Tuesday 15 August

I have a nice house at Gorleston on Sea, near the golf course. The house (a bungalow) costs me 25 guineas a week. When I have my family with me – Joan, Gail and Gary – then I don't think the price is too much, but when I'm alone, which I am for seven weeks out of the thirteen, then it's a lot to pay.[1] Living near the golf course here, as I do, and Jimmy Lee, my dresser, playing golf, I thought I'd take the game up[2]. About two weeks ago I was playing golf with Jimmy and Bob and Alf Pearson[3] when Bob mentioned the name of a double act they once worked with: Joan Stonehewer and Walter Bracegirdle. Well, when I heard that name I flipped. To me that is one of the funniest names ever. I shall have to use it on TV or in a film.

I see the house full boards are outside ABC Theatre. We are doing well but not well enough. Not capacity bizz. Very good bizz but not full and I'm afraid on our salary we should be. But I'm not making any excuses. The Grades[4] have put the prices up this season, as they now do in every town we play. Last year the top price was 10/6 per seat. This year it's 12/6 – two shillings extra, and the 12/6 seats go back to four rows from the back, which are 10/6. But the way things are going should average £8000 a week for the Grades for thirteen weeks which is a lot of money! I feel that Joan is getting bored with being here, although Gail and Gary are both good kids. But the weather has broken and as Joan says, 'What can you do? It's dull.' True!

Rare photographic evidence that Eric did indeed, on at least one occasion, actually make a cup of tea. His mother Sadie looks suitably surprised, if not ecstatic.

While we have been doing the show at Yarmouth we have put some new bits in – the ventriloquist routine and the Spanish dance that we did on TV here and in the States. Both have done well but the ventriloquist routine is great. It's the best bit of material we have had for five to ten years. We must keep it off TV. The Spanish dance went well but somehow it wasn't a Yarmouth bit. Now that the show has been on a few weeks we have made it more basic, which is really a pity. You have to make these type of people laugh with blueness. It can take away the humour out of a good bit.

Albert Saveen[5] is on at the moment and his laughs are: 'my wife's an angel – you're lucky, mine's still living,' and, 'a woman comes into a man's life like a ray of sunshine, and goes through his pockets like a streak of lightning.' This to me is sickening because I knew Albert twenty years ago and he's still doing the same thing. It's very sad.

It's funny really, talking about Albert, but he came to see me a few minutes ago. He's using a dog in his act and the old dog he used to have in his act died this morning. I didn't know if I should laugh or not. His dog was 15 years old, which shows how long he's been doing the dog bit.

1 Eric was in good company. The house had previously been rented by the celebrated crooner Matt Monro, and subsequently by the comedian Dickie Henderson, who gave the main address at Eric's funeral.

2 Eric became quite good at golf, but although he enjoyed a round or two, he never took the game too seriously. 'Golf is a wonderful sport,' he used to say, 'especially if your wife won't let you drink at home.' 'Eric hated golf club snobbery,' says Gary. 'He'd play so-called friends and just to make it interesting, they'd put a few bob on it. But then if he won, there was this angst afterwards – bad feeling and tension. He thought, "How bloody stupid! It's a game!"'

3 Alf Pearson and his brother Bob were a popular singing duo: 'We bring you melodies from out of the sky, my brother and I.'

4 Lew Grade, Leslie Grade and their brother Bernard Delfont were the undisputed first family of British Light Entertainment.

5 Veteran ventriloquist Albert Saveen cultivated his vocal skills by learning to use his lungs alternately, as he recuperated in hospital after suffering respiratory damage during World War Two. Saveen had more than a dozen puppets, including an East End lad called Andy the Spiv and a schoolgirl called Daisy May: 'Daisy May, people say you'll marry me one day, and by the way you sigh, and look me in the eye, somehow I think that Daisy may.'

Wednesday 16 August

This morning I played golf with Arthur Askey[1]. I lost every hole – but at least I didn't cheat, which in itself must be a record[2]. It's about three weeks since we heard from Billy Marsh[3]. He's suddenly gone very quiet. Nothing office wise has happened since we refused the Palladium Panto. The offer was two fold: around £4000 a week or £3000 with a cut in the take. It would run for about twenty weeks. For the season it would work out at £90,000. They can't understand that we would turn down so much money. But it takes guts or ignorance turning that kind of money down. Just writing about it and my hand goes shaky. I bet they come back with some other offer, but we must wait to see if anything happens Stateside. The reason we still turned it down is because we have just finished a colour TV series for the States[4]. It's the first one ever to be done over here. All British made and, as far as one can say, it's been a success so we must wait to see what develops from it. It could be nothing, but for heaven's sake one has to gamble sometime. In the end that £90,000 could be peanuts, but it's gone now.

Out front tonight, first house, is Phillip Jones, an ABC TV producer. He'll come round later. Good idea to get him to offer us a series via the Grades, then see what happens. I'd bet the offer would never get to us.[5] Both houses tonight are full but the weather at the moment is good theatre weather.[6] Friday and Saturday first houses could let us down and stop us from doing a buster – £9,900. I think we might do around £9,500 this week.

As for Yarmouth itself, although I'm making a lot of money here, I think Yarmouth is really a most terrible place. If cleanliness is next to godliness, in Yarmouth it's next to impossible. Just outside the ABC stage door is a market, and at the end of the day there is so much paper and old fish and chips, as there are about six fish, chip and pea stalls belching out terrible smells eighteen hours a day. But the public put up with all this dirt and smells. I've been reading in the papers lately about how dirty the British are. It seems to be true in Yarmouth.

1 Pint sized comedian Arthur Askey was Eric and Ernie's comic idol. Ernie appeared with Askey in Variety before he teamed up with Eric, but the fact that Askey had now become Eric's golfing buddy showed how far Morecambe & Wise had come.

2 'Eric's temperament wasn't made for golf because you have one great day and one bad day, or one great shot and one bad shot, and that used to put him in such a bad mood,' says Gary. 'I walked round with him lots of times on the course. When it was going well, it was going well – but when it wasn't, we all knew about it, so he wasn't cut out for it. It wasn't doing him any good.' As Eric's chauffeur, Mike Fountain, says, 'He enjoyed the walk rather than the golfing.'

3 Billy Marsh was Eric and Ernie's agent from 1959. Having worked for Bernard Delfont since 1942, he went on to launch London Management with Delfont's nephew, Michael Grade. His many famous clients have included Bruce Forsyth and Norman Wisdom.

4 Entitled The Piccadilly Palace, this series was transmitted in the United States by ABC TV (as a summer stand in for another ABC show called The Hollywood Palace) and subsequently broadcast on ITV as Eric and Ernie's sixth (and final) series for ATV. 'They went down pretty well,' says Joan, 'but the trouble was, in the States they cut them all to pieces because of their advertising.' The show was videotaped on the NTSC system (given the mnemonic Never The Same Colour, due to technical problems) to be shown in 'living' colour in the States, but when it was repeated in Britain it was screened in plain old black and white. Eric and Ernie's impatience (and ATV's reluctance) to switch to colour was a significant factor in their subsequent move to the BBC.

5 Ernie is usually credited as the business brains behind the partnership, but Eric's scheming shows a cunning showbiz mind at work.

6 By 'good theatre weather', Eric meant lousy weather for the rest of us. Good weather has always meant bad business for theatricals, and it was especially important for seaside shows like these. There was no air conditioning in those days, and when the sun shone, holidaymakers would linger on the beach or prom, rather than seeking shelter in the theatres. Indeed, Britain's notoriously unpredictable climate was a key factor in the development of British seaside comedy, and British seaside comics like Eric. Elsewhere, the weather was too good to tempt audiences indoors.

Thursday 17 August

Took the family to Norwich this morning for a drive. Had lunch at the Bell hotel. The food was fair, but when you look at the waiters in their ill-fitting suits full of soup stains it really is terrible. How an overseas visitor must feel I don't know. If only we could get like America in this respect. No one seems to care. I suppose I should complain but I'm a coward. I seem to be on the dirt kick at the moment but it is true. I took my mother and father to the railway station here about three weeks ago. Not one porter offered to help with the bags. The train was dirty, but I didn't say anything. One seems to get a take it or leave it attitude from staff these days.

Played golf with Jimmy Lee and Alf Pearson. I played terrible. Had lunch at home. My dear wife is not too well after her operation, but we can only hope that all has gone well. Ninety-two stitches in her legs and thighs. She's really wonderful the way she's taking these things in her stride (if you'll excuse the pun).[1]

Had a film script sent to me by Cyril Coke[2] called Mr Mercury. Although the start and the first three or four pages were great, the rest ran to the same pattern as our last three films, so I wrote to him last night and told him it wasn't what we wanted. George Bartram[3] came to see us with a clipping book. It's amazing how the last film we did is doing such great bizz.[4]

Tonight is the midnight matinee. We will be doing the bongos and the ventriloquist routine. I'm trying to stop cigs by smoking my pipe. I have a slight pain on the left side around the heart. It's most likely wind, but I've had it for about four days. That's a hell of a time to have wind.[5] We received some nice mail from America today. They seem to like the show.

1 Joan was recovering from an operation to remove varicose veins.

2 Cyril Coke had directed the ITV sitcom Our Man At St Marks, starring Leslie Phillips and Donald Sinden, for Associated Rediffusion. He also did more highbrow work, such as adapting Arthur Koestler's Darkness At Noon. He had a holiday home in Portugal and it was on his advice that Eric bought a plot of land and built a villa over there. However although Coke sent Eric several film scripts down the years, Eric didn't feel that any of them were right for him and Ernie.

3 George Bartram was Eric and Ernie's enterprising publicist.

4 There's no accounting for public taste. The film in question was the inappropriately entitled The Magnificent Two.

5 Eric was a chronic hypochondriac, but it was rare for him to commit his health worries to paper. Was this a premonition of his impending heart attack?

Sunday 20 August

Did the midnight show two nights ago. We did well, but I told Ernie that I don't think we should do any more of them. They are too competitive. One has to make all sorts of conditions regards where one is played on the programme, and quite naturally the younger less known comic is trying to prove to the people how much better they are than the more well known comics. The same thing arises with singers. The whole affair ends up as a 'who's best?' The idea that it's a charity show done for nothing somehow gets lost on the way. It just isn't worth doing. Arthur Askey has the right idea. He just says no thank you!

Had a nice quiet weekend. Played a good game of golf Sunday night. Also today with the usual three – Jim Lee, Bob and Alf Pearson. It seems very hot today so I should think working will be sweaty. Also I think the good weather will knock off a bit bizz wise tonight. Had a short letter from Billy Marsh – about time. Still no news about America.

Wednesday 23 August

Bought a watch the other day. It does everything which is a pity as there are still one or two things I'd like to do myself. Paid £38/16-0 for it. It's called a Breitling. Played golf this morning and won a ball. Bizz still seems to be holding up although the weather is great. Tomorrow Jimmy Lee has fixed up some trout fishing so we'll see if I'm lucky. Just had a look back in this book. My scrawl, that's all I can call it, is shocking. I must try to do better.

Bought Gail another horse today – 200 guineas. Part exchanged Autumn Lady for £130. Autumn Lady cost £155. The new horse is or seems to be a much better one and seems to be a lot more friendly. Gail will be upset at Autumn Lady going but she wants this one badly, so I think she will soon get over it. She seems to be very good with horses. Gary seems the one to be more upset although he couldn't care less about horses. Kids are strange.

Monday 28 August

Yesterday went to Peterfield House Hotel at Horning. Took Joan and family, Pat and Amanda [family friends], Arthur Askey. Met Val Doonican and Lyn[1], plus Mike Grade and Penny [Grade's first wife]. Had a glorious day as the weather was great. The food was excellent. Finished up at five o'clock with tea and champagne on the lawn. Gail and Gary were extra well behaved and Gail has got to the age where she can join in with the grown ups and hold her own.

Brian Epstein[2] was found dead yesterday. How terrible. How very sad. A young man who on the surface had everything to live for. It's supposed to have been an overdose – accidental, or otherwise? I suppose we will never know. Somehow, to me, these people like the Beatles, Mick Jagger and the like, now that they have this fantastic money seem to be looking for something else – but what they're looking for isn't there. I never knew Epstein but I knew the Beatles[3]. I hope they stop all this foolishness and live normal lives.

1 Val Doonican's wife, the entertainer Lynnette Rae.

2 Brian Epstein managed the Beatles from 1961 until his death in 1967. The coroner recorded a verdict of accidental death from 'incautious self-overdoses.' Despite his prematurely middle aged appearance, he was just 32.

3 The Beatles appeared on Eric and Ernie's ATV show in April 1964, soon after the release of their chart topping single, Can't Buy Me Love.

Wednesday 30 August

Played golf again today. Played very well. Won a ball. Colin Clews[1] is going to arrive later this evening. We will talk over the editing of the American series[2], as they will come out in this country, but we have the proviso of editing because some of it has been seen here before. It's strange really how the Grade Organisation are quite willing to let the shows go out as they are, which proves they are not interested in us. It's a damn good job we had so much put in the contract, otherwise they would crucify us.

1 Colin Clews produced Eric and Ernie's show for ATV. He also produced Dave Allen, Marty Feldman, Larry Grayson, Sid James, Jimmy Tarbuck, Des O'Connor and Mike & Bernie Winters.

2 The Piccadilly Palace, broadcast in the United States by ABC, and later shown on ITV as Eric and Ernie's final series for ATV.

Monday 4 September

Played golf well this morning but got no proof as I played alone. This is the week that I think the bizz will drop but we have to wait and see. The town itself is only half full and there's plenty of room for cars, which is always a sure sign.

Thursday 7 September

I was so tired last night, I slept for ten hours. For three days now we have had a reporter from the TV Times with us, for an article[1]. It's for the front cover in colour for our States shows when they are shown here in October. Dick and Pam Hills[2] are coming tonight, so we should learn a few things of what's been going on, on the TV scene.

1 Eric and Ernie always recognised the immense value of good publicity, and were uniquely accommodating to the press. 'It never went to their heads, being stars,' says Joan. 'They would always talk to anybody.'

2 With Sid Green, Dick Hills wrote (and appeared in) six series of the Morecambe & Wise Show for ATV, plus Eric and Ernie's first series at the BBC. They were also employed as scriptwriters on Eric and Ernie's three feature films.

Friday 8 September

Went out last night with Dick and Pam Hills, Ern and Dorothy and Roger Hancock, Tony's brother. There was a lot of laughs going. I think Dick and Pam are getting very fed up with Sid. We all had dinner at The Star, where Dick said that Sid was retiring. We laughed at that. I think it's all his domestic troubles. Mind you it wouldn't surprise me, knowing Sid to be a stubborn thing! I bet he will be out of retirement within three weeks. Well, it's stupid – he's only thirty-nine, and I'm sure he can't be all that well off. It takes a hell of a lot of money to retire today. I must have near a hundred grand if I sold out, but I couldn't retire and live the way I would like to live. I think Sid will get over it, if he has any sense that is.

Saturday 9 September

I wrote to Sid and told him to have a good rest as he has been working very hard lately. He's written our last film, then the American series we did, then on to the Bruce Forsyth Show, without a stop. So the man must be tired, but I hope he hasn't snapped. Anyway I still think after a good rest he'll be back, but it was quite sad to read the letter.

Monday 11 September

Last night I saw a great film, Doctor Zhivago. I took the family and was very pleased that Gail and Gary sat through the whole film, and although it was a slow love story (which I don't think is them yet!) they were very good. Both Joan and I thought it really was excellent. Joan leaves on Wednesday to take the kiddies back to Harpenden. I shall miss them very much, but it will only be for one and a half weeks, then I will be in our new home. I'm dying to see the house with the extension on. It should make it look so big. Joan doesn't like the existing name because it reminds her of Morris, the man we bought it off, so I think we will call it Little Paddock for obvious reasons.

I came to the theatre at five o'clock, and there waiting were two American girls. They had come all the way from Rochester, New Jersey, for five days in London, and they had seen all our shows on TV in the States, and, very happy to say, they are great fans of ours. So they found out where Great Yarmouth is (a feat in itself) and came along to see the show, all the way from New Jersey. They are out front in this audience at the moment and seem to be enjoying it very much!

Wednesday 13 September

Joan and the children left at 10.30 this morning for home (Harpenden). The car was so full of stuff, if they ever have a puncture they will be able to set up shop on the roadside. I rang Joan at four this afternoon and was pleased to hear her. She had arrived safe and sound, glad to say, but the new house was in a shambles and Joan has blown her top. But you can't blame her. I hope things work out soon. She has no lights, there was no carpet down and it was filthy. What with her leaving me here – the house is like a morgue – and getting home to find the new house in that condition. On her arrival the house was in a terrible state, but Joan and Betty (the daily) set about it, and within a few hours time it was still in a terrible state – but habitable. What a wonderful woman she is, even though she does get on to me at times.

Thursday 14 September

Gail's birthday. Happy birthday darling. Fourteen years old. Times goes so quickly. I feel as if I can remember every day of her life. She's a wonderful daughter and if she wasn't a little lazy, she could be a very clever one. The trouble is, she takes after me. It's nice to have a son and daughter, and they are both good children. I think I must be one of the luckiest men alive! I've got a wonderful wife and two great children, houses, a hotel, money, almost everything. Sometimes it worries me. I feel something's got to give. I know what Harry Secombe[1] meant when he said he's worried that one day the phone will ring and a very mystic voice will say, 'Thank you, Mr Secombe. Now can we have it all back?'

1 Like Eric, Harry Secombe cut his comic teeth at the Windmill Theatre, before finding fame on The Goon Show alongside Spike Milligan, Peter Sellers and Michael Bentine.

Tuesday 19 September

Went home at the weekend. Started off at 7am. Two hours, 25 minutes. The new house is going to look fine. As I travelled from Yarmouth, it was dull and misty, and as I got to Harpenden the sun shone and it made the house look wonderful. It felt like an omen.

Monday 25 September

Well, that's another season over and done with. On the whole it's been a very happy one. I have never in 27 years of showbiz seen so many people cry at the end of a show so much. One expects the girls to have a little cry, but even the men were filling up. Over the season it made £105,640, which although it broke all other records was not enough. Billy Marsh said that after all had been paid – £39,000 to us, the rest of the show, the theatre percentages, etc, Leslie Grade made £1000. Leslie didn't make money this time, but that's the gamble they take. They must have made a fortune at Blackpool out of us in 65 – £165,000 at much less money for us. Poor Lew and Leslie!

I came home after the show on Saturday. Started at ten past eleven, arrived at 2am. Joan was up waiting for me and I had a meal. What a wonderful woman. It's a dull day today but great to be home, even though things are chaotic. I went to the golf club today (as the new house is on the thirteenth). I've already made an application to become a general member. I went round the course and it is beautiful. The house looks great from the course.

Sunday 15 October

Arrived back from Portugal, and our villa over there is in a worse state than the house over here. Somehow you can't win. The weather was very nice – in the eighties. We met some very nice people – all were charming and live in the Algarve. But I feel that most of the other residents are mostly failures over here. They only seem to be scratching a living over there. They are the ones who say, 'Isn't the weather wonderful? You can't get this at home. You won't get me going back.' Not unless they are deported, and I feel some of them will be! At the moment I'm one of those unfashionable people who happen to love England. It's great to be back – weather and all.

Sunday 29 October

The other day I bought a book on British birds and found it most interesting. I sit by the lounge window with the field glasses and bird watch. I've made a list at the back of the birds I've seen so far in my garden.

Friday 24 November

New York. My God, it's weeks since I wrote anything in this book. I've had all the time in the world in which to do it, as since I finished Yarmouth I've done absolutely nothing. One record[1] and two interviews with BBC Radio. The shows that we did for the States are now coming out every three weeks in Britain. The first one got number one in the ratings. The second one came in at number five and the third one came in at number one again. It will be interesting to work out the average when the States is over.

It's nine o'clock in the morning, the day after Thanksgiving Day. I'm having my Continental breakfast in my room – the New York Hilton, which is not a hotel I would stay at again. I prefer the Americana, or the others I've stayed in. Ern and me are over here to do a Sullivan[2] show this Sunday.

1 The record was Twelve Days of Christmas, released as a single by Pye.

2 For a more detailed account of Eric and Ernie's appearances on the Ed Sullivan Show, see Chapter Six.

Monday 27 November

New York. Ernie's birthday. I haven't as yet bought him anything, but will probably buy him something small, like a small TV set (joke). Did the show last night – OK, but really it's like hitting your head against a brick wall. This can do us not much good. But the money is good – $9000, with tips (joke).

Tuesday 28 November

New York. Today we saw Billy Marsh, who came over to see us and Norman Wisdom. He told me Jock Cochrane, an old friend of mine, died in England last week. Early in our career he did a lot for us. This afternoon, Billy, Ern and me went to the Sullivan office to have a talk with Bob Precht, who is Ed's booking manager. He was happy with the show we did and would like us to do as many more as we want. So it looks like we will be back again in the New Year. He also mentioned a Broadway show[1], but this is in the very early talking stage as yet. Billy is by devious ways trying to get us to do as much over here as possible, but I think it's only to make gains for his own end.

1 Eric and Ernie never did get to do their own show on Broadway, but after they died, a play about them, The Play What I Wrote, transferred there from London's West End.

Monday 11 December

Harpenden. At the moment it is snowing. The ground is all covered. It looks very nice, but it's caused chaos on the roads and rail. As always when this country gets a few inches of snow – chaos. If I didn't know better, places like Norway and Sweden must be in a permanent state of chaos.

I came back from Leicester this morning where I did a Sunday concert. It went very well and was, I think, a great try out for the club next week. Today is our wedding anniversary. I bought Joan a nice card and a bowl of flowers. It looks great. I go to see Mr Philip Lawton tomorrow regards tax. He is supposed to be one of the top three tax lawyers in the country. I hope so.

Friday 22 December

Leeds. Queens Hotel. We have nearly finished our week at the club at Batley[1]. It's gone great. The place itself holds 1700 people and it's been sold out for the week. Although we have done really well, I somehow don't think this type of work is the best for us. It's too much working class – pints and big men – and they can be a bit rowdy. But it's been an important exercise. We average between 45 and 60 minutes – £4000 this week.

1 It was back at Batley the following year that Eric suffered his first heart attack.

Sunday 31 December

New Year's Eve. I am full of a cold. Also there is an epidemic of flu going around at the moment. I think mine is just a head cold. It's the first cold I've had for over eighteen months. We threw a small house warming party last Friday. Morris and Marg came. They are the people we bought this house off. They were amazed at the extras we've had and are still having done. Next week off to New York again. I'm not looking forward to it, but I never do. Sometimes I think there must be something wrong with me.

The closest Eric ever got to being in his own swimming pool. This dinghy bit the dust when Eric fell asleep in it. His pipe burnt a hole in it and, with a loud farting noise, it rapidly began to sink. Eric couldn't swim, but his cries for help alerted his son Gary, whose prompt rescue (while trying valiantly to suppress a fit of giggles) saved Eric from a watery grave.

Chapter 14

THE DIARIES 1968

Thursday 4 January

Well here I go again – off to the States. How can I explain the feeling I get? Sometimes I hate flying, I even hate going, and yet I enjoy the whole thing. I suppose it's a love hate relationship. Thirty five thousand feet up, so the pilot said, and I'm not going to argue with him. At this moment I'm in a Boeing 707 flying first class over the Atlantic to New York. Ernie and I are going to do a show on TV for Ed Sullivan. This is now the tenth show we have done for Sullivan in America. Brian [Eric's occasional chauffeur] took me to the airport this morning. Gary, my son, and Clive, my nephew, came to Heathrow to see me off. Really they don't come to wish me a safe trip. They come to see the planes. Although Gary has seen me off many times, this is the first time I saw him from the plane. He was wearing his light blue jeans and short anorak, so I just looked for a pair of light blue jeans and a pasty face.

Although I'm not keen on flying, I must say I enjoy the trip. Mind you, I do get very good treatment. I'm met at Heathrow by PanAm reps and whisked off to a little room used only by special people. Also I'm met at Kennedy by more PanAm reps and taken through very quickly. On these PanAm planes you are well looked after. You get a very good meal, all you can drink and a film show. For the film show you do have to pay a pound extra, but it helps to pass the seven to eight hour trip. On this journey it will take eight hours, which for 3000 odd miles can't be bad. When I arrived, I took a cab to my hotel. Although American hotels are very good, the room I'm in isn't. It's costing me $26 a day, then there's food on top of that. I met Ernie but I was so tired I felt ill, so we just had a drink together and I went back to the hotel. I was in bed at 9.30pm. It has just started to snow.

Friday 5 January

Waldorf Astoria, New York. Got up this morning at 9.30 – fifteen degrees below freezing. I went downstairs from the 21st floor and took a walk around the block, then had breakfast. This afternoon, Ern and I went to the Sullivan office to have a talk through with the producer. He was quite happy with the bit we were going to do. It's late afternoon – cocktail hour, which I am all for. Had a couple of drinks at the Essex House, where Ernie is staying, then back to the hotel[1]. Watched some TV, which if you compare it with British TV, well to me they know nothing. Went and ate. Bed early.

1 Eric and Ernie stayed in separate hotels when they were away working. Yet far from betraying any animosity between them, this arrangement helped to keep their relationship in tip top form.

Top: **If we can make it there, we'll make it anywhere... Eric & Ernie hit New York for an appearance on the Ed Sullivan Show. Left to Right: Ernie's wife Doreen, Eric, Eric's wife Joan, Ernie and co-writer of their ATV shows Sid Green. Sid's writing partner, Dick Hills, took the photo.**

Left: **So good they named it twice. Eric and Joan in New York, on their way to meet Ed Sullivan.**

Below: **Eric taking tea, Liberace style.**

Saturday 6 January

Waldorf Astoria, New York. Today is a hard day. Two or three run throughs at the theatre, now called the Ed Sullivan Theatre, on Broadway. Then a quick lunch and a music run in the afternoon. Saw the name Morecambe & Wise on the front of the theatre – first time on Broadway. Mind you, it won't be there for long. We do the show tomorrow, so it will be taken down tomorrow night. Got back to the hotel and the phone is flashing. It's Fred Harris, an Englishman who works in New York for the Grade Delfont office. We stayed in the Waldorf for drinks as it was too cold to go out. We got slowly pissed, then went and had a bowl of soup downstairs in the café. This would be 12.30am. I then said, 'Goodnight.' He didn't speak, got a cab and went home. I went back to my furnace of a room and fell asleep. I didn't even switch on the TV.

Sunday 7 January

Waldorf Astoria, New York, It's thick snow outside. It's thick hammers inside my head. However it's show time this morning – got to get down to the Sullivan Theatre for 9.15am. Now to try and be funny at that time in the morning – believe me, there's no such time. But it's got to be done. This trip the weather has been really cold – fifteen below. I hope the plane will take off tomorrow. It could have cleared by then. Ern and I do the Sullivan again tonight. We will do the Marvo & Dolores bit.[1] All the crew think it's very funny. I think it will die, but I have been wrong before. We rehearse and hang about the theatre all day. Fred comes round before the show. The show is over, they say it's gone well. I'm not happy about it, nor is the Boy Wonder,[2] but they are – so much so, Ed asks us out to dinner with him that night. We go to Danny's Hideaway on Lexington and have a very informal and most enjoyable evening. Bed around 12am.

1 Marvo & Dolores was Eric and Ernie's spoof magic act, with Eric as a cod magician, and Ernie as his (none too) glamorous assistant.

2 The Boy Wonder was Eric's pet name for Ernie.

Monday 8 January

Waldorf Astoria, New York. Well, I'm going back home tonight – back to the 35,000 feet up again bit, and this time I'm not sorry[1]. It's 29 degrees below freezing, and that to me is cold. I'm going tonight on the ten o'clock flight from New York, but this time it's BOAC. I've checked out of the hotel and took all my cases to the Essex House. Taxi at 7.15, airport at eight, VIP room 8.30, 9.15 not drunk but happy. Great. Thirty five thousand feet up again, on the way home. Did the Sullivan last night, and did well – maybe the best we have done. In a few moments the pilot has asked me to go up front while we are landing. This should be a thrill.

1 Eric's determination to fly straight home as soon as they'd finished the show was one of the main reasons why Morecambe & Wise never became big stars in the States. 'He liked to get home as soon as possible,' says Joan. 'Ernie was very relaxed, and he'd treat it more as a holiday. Eric could never really relax if he was working.'

Tuesday 9 January

Home again – great to see Joan and the kids. I went to bed to catch up on the lost – or gained (I never know which) hours, so I slept nearly all day. Just before we reached London Airport, I was asked by the pilot if I would like to sit in on the landing. It was a great experience as the whole country was in the overnight grip of a very heavy snowstorm. I was allowed to put on the headphones and listen to all the other planes asking where to land as London Airport would have only one strip open, and they were not sure what time that would be. So planes ahead of us were being sent to Frankfurt and Prestwick and Paris, but we were rather lucky in as much as the strip was open at 11.30 and we had only stacked for fifteen to twenty minutes. All the planes in front had stacked for much longer, and had all made decisions to fly elsewhere, so ours was the first plane in.

Wednesday 10 January

Just hung about the house.

Thursday 11 January

Very little happening. Wrote a script. Could be quite funny.

Friday 12 January

Nothing. Wrote a script. Haven't finished it. Can't get a good enough tag.

Saturday 13 January

Watched TV sport. Nothing else.

Sunday 14 January

All this time wasting is getting me down. I just seem to hang around the house all day, then at night time I sit watching TV. I've been back home since last Tuesday, and done nothing. I'm getting a little worried about the weight I'm putting on – and the laziness regards getting it off. I would think I'm about a stone overweight. I weighed myself today – 12 stone 4 lbs. When I was married fifteen years ago, I was 9 stone 10 lbs. Some of it has to come off. I must get down to about 11 stone.

Monday 15 January

Started on a diet. Black coffee, lemon tea and bread (starch reduced). No fry-ups (sad). Ernie phoned – going to the office tomorrow.

Tuesday 16 January

Today I went to the Delfont Grade office in Regent Street to meet Ernie and Billy Marsh. We had a long chat about future deals. I mentioned a tax saving scheme to Ernie and was rather surprised that he seemed quite interested, as since we have been married we have kept everything separate, and now Ernie is so close with information I never know what he is doing. All he does is secret! The idea is that we should both take out a policy on each other for £4,000 pa for ten years and after the ten years are up, for the next five years we are paid back at so much a year. At the end of the five years we will get £72,000 each – that of course is with profits. The beauty of it is that the £4,000 pa comes out of our different companies. If it comes out of the profits you are not taxed on the £4,000 at all. The only time you are taxed is when you start earning on the five yearly payments and by then we will have retired and will not be in the same earning capacity as we are now, so the tax will be less than now. I left the thought with the Boy Wonder, and I'll wait to hear from him regards it, although I don't think he will want to come across[1]. Also if one of us dies, the other gets it, and Ern doesn't look too well. It's all a matter of pushing the money I'm earning now into the future.

Had lunch with Leslie Grade at Dickins & Jones. Very interesting as Leslie, who is a very shrewd man, had one or two propositions to offer – but with Leslie you have to think everything over for two or three days. Then you end up with the answer, which is nearly always, 'Well, where does Leslie's share come in?' But it's in there somewhere!

1 Ernie did insure himself against injury to Eric, but he let the policy lapse just before Eric's first heart attack.

Thursday 18 January

Today I was asked to become President of Kimpton Players. It sounds like a football team, but it's a group of amateur actors and actresses who do local shows for charity. It should be quite interesting. They are doing an old time music hall show in a few weeks time, so I'll be getting a party together and going along.

Ern and I had a meeting with our writers, Sid Green and Dick Hills, at Roger Hancock's office. We went to talk over a film idea for this coming summer. After a few drinks, conversation loosened up and Sid and Dick came out with the idea of doing a film about gypsies, where Ern and I are something to do with the council, and we have the job of moving them on, off the land that they are on. Although they had a few good situations within the film I could see Ern was not too happy about it, and I must admit I wasn't jumping for joy. It's a good idea, but it's an idea anyone could do. It's not pure Morecambe & Wise. Over lunch I happened to mention an offbeat idea I had for a film, which all thought funny. At that point Sid said that if that was the type of film we were thinking in terms of, he was all for it. So it looks as if we may after all be doing a type of film that we are all keen to do. The boys went off to write it up. We meet again next week.

Friday 19 January

Home all day.

Saturday 20 January

TV sport.

Sunday 21 January

Had a change – stayed home!

Monday 22 January

Just rang a few friends who are working. I'm quite jealous.

Tuesday 23 January

I took Joan out to see Fiddler on The Roof this evening. It was a very good show. The Jewish actor Topol was the lead and he was excellent. Really it's a one man show with about eighty in the cast, but it is very good.

Wednesday 24 January

Nothing.

Thursday 25 January

Met Sid and Dick this morning for lunch. They had worked out a rough idea on the film. It was good.[1]

1 In the event, Eric and Ernie never made another big screen film with Sid and Dick – or with anyone else, for that matter.

Friday 26 January

Home all day. Mind you, I went out yesterday.

Saturday 27 January

This evening Joan and I went to the Drysdales [family friends] for drinks, before going on to the golf club. Met Enid and Mike Price (my doctor). Made arrangement to play golf this Tuesday and to go out on Tuesday evening, as they are going to see Sweet Charity at the same time as us. Both Mike and Enid were suffering from some sort of flu.

Sunday 28 January

My mother and father arrived this afternoon from Morecambe. Jack Ashworth, my auditor, brought them down. Great to see them. My father looks younger than me! And I know he's older! Also Sadie looks so well[1]. I hope they keep it up. The rest of the day was taken up with tax, insurance, etc. It's difficult to realise when they say £50,000 there, £25,000 for each of the kids, £72,000 when you're sixty. It's hard to realise they are talking about MY money.

1 Eric's father, George, died in 1976, followed by his mother, Sadie, in 1977.

Monday 29 January

Jack and myself went to see three insurance people at their office in Gracechurch Street to talk over an idea Jack has re pushing money into the future. We have to wait now to see what the Inland Revenue think about it. I'm worried about it, as we are so near March 19 – tax day. I think the revenue people will hold back on any scheme at the moment. Went to PanAm for my air tickets for the States on Wednesday. Met one of their top men, and he took us out to lunch at the Playboy Club. Came home. Went to bed at ten. I feel very bad. I think I've got this virus or flu that Mike and Enid had.

Tuesday 30 January

When I got up this morning I felt bad, but I had to play a game of golf with Mike Price, so this afternoon we played and we won. I must say I felt better for playing, and much better for winning. This evening Joan and I drove into London to see a very good show with Muriel Young[1]. It was at the Prince of Wales Theatre, and the show was called Sweet Charity. It really was excellent. After the show we met Mike and Enid Price for dinner with Muriel. We ate in a little Italian restaurant in Romilly Street. Also excellent, but I think I had a little too much wine. In the night I was sick, but I would say that got rid of the virus.

1 Muriel Young was a children's television presenter and producer, and the wife of TV drama director Cyril Coke, Eric's neighbour in the Algarve.

Wednesday 31 January

New York. Brian came this morning to take me to the airport. It was a very nice trip – just seven and a half hours. I was met at airport by Fred Harris. Bought him a bottle of Glenfiddich Scotch, which is his favourite. He seemed very pleased. Fred has fixed me up at the Hotel Meurice. I don't know how Fred does it – $16 a day for a suite. For New York prices, as Fred says, it's the best bargain in town. It's a little old fashioned, but at least you can walk about in it. I had arranged for the helicopter to take us into New York, on top of the Pan Am building. It was a bit shaky. I don't think I'd do it again. It's a fantastic sight flying over New York in the daylight, but I'm told it's even better to fly over on a clear night. However I don't fancy it. It didn't feel safe to me, and it didn't look safe either.

Thursday 1 February

New York. We went to the Sullivan office today to meet the girl who is doing the wall bit with us. She's called Michelle Lee. She was in the Broadway show of How To Succeed[1] and also in the film. She is very pretty and also is keen to do it (the bit, I mean). She's very good, and we took to each other right away, which is good when you're working together. Bob Precht, Sullivan's director, asked us if we would stay over until the weekend, to do another show on Saturday. It's a tribute for Irving Berlin's 80th birthday, so we said we would. It's also with Bing Crosby and Bob Hope.

1 The show's full title was How To Succeed In Business Without Really Trying.

Friday 2 February

New York. Went out to the Playboy Club with Fred last night to have a look at a comic called George Weston. I didn't rate him and the customers didn't either. Fred liked him. Poor Fred. Although it was a free night, the food was terrible. This morning we rehearsed the wall routine. Started at 10.30, finished two o'clock. This afternoon came back to my suite and had an hour's rest on the bed. Went out around four and bought one of those thick newspapers, a carton of Vitamin D milk (that makes me laugh) and three bananas. That's lunch taken care of.

Saturday 3 February

Rehearsed all day, with Michelle. Went to bed early without Michelle!

Sunday 4 February

New York. The day of the show. Nine fifteen at the theatre, saw our name outside. I must say it gives on a kick to see your name up on Broadway. At nine thirty we had a music call, then did what the Americans call blocking, which is a camera run through. Back at twelve in the afternoon for make up. At one o'clock, a complete dress run with people out front. It went very well. They had no notes for us. Next show would be show time at eight o'clock. Eight o'clock till nine o'clock – the show, which was great for us. It really did go well. Best we have ever done here.

After the show Janet Munro[1] who is Ian Hendry's[2] wife, came to see us with her father[3]. They enjoyed it and are also big fans. Janet phoned Ian that afternoon, and told him she was going to see us. He said he was watching us at home in England, while she was phoning. Also met Vincent Price[4] and Pat Routledge[5]. Both very nice people. Pat and Vincent are doing a show on Broadway called Darling of The Day. I'm told she is great but the show isn't!

1 Janet Munro was a British actress who appeared in Walt Disney movies like Swiss Family Robinson and British feature films such as The Day The Earth Caught Fire.

2 Munro's husband, British actor Ian Hendry, was the original star of The Avengers, opposite Patrick MacNee. He later appeared in several classic British movies, alongside Michael Caine in Get Carter and Sean Connery in The Hill.

3 Janet's father, Alex Munro, was a seasoned Scottish comic.

4 One of America's finest horror movie actors, Vincent Price starred in creepy camp classics such as House of Wax and The Fall of The House of Usher.

5 British actress Patricia Routledge, nowadays best known as suburban snob Hyacinth Bucket (pronounced 'Bouquet') in Roy Clarke's brilliant BBC sitcom, Keeping Up Appearances.

Monday 5 February

New York. I didn't do much today. I got up late, and had lunch at a Chinese restaurant. People knew me from the show the night before. I felt like walking about saying, 'Yes, I was on last night. Oh! So glad you liked it!' However one can't do that, although I know one or two people who almost do. I stayed in most of the afternoon. Fred rang up at about five and came over to the hotel about six thirty. He had nothing lined up so he rang the George Abbott Theatre to see if he could walk over and get tickets for Darling of The Day. It was very easy, so we went. The theatre was half full (a pessimist would say half empty). Pat was very good but the show was lacking somewhere. Mind you, that is always easy to say. I know I couldn't have put it right. After the show Fred and I went and had a bowl of soup at some Broadway café. Home then, and a few drinks and kip.

Tuesday 6 February

New York. This morning I had to meet Pat Kilburn (an old Harpenden friend) in Saks on Fifth Avenue, or as the Americans say, Fitavenooo. Pat came at eleven as arranged. Pat wanted to shop and buy some shoes and a matching handbag, which we did. I noticed while waiting for Pat in the shoe shop that the American women treat the sellers like dirt. To me they do have a class distinction, but it's all of their own, and comes mostly from women. The more I'm over here the more I'm glad I'm English – British even. Pat and I went to the top of the Pan Am for a quiet drink, which in New York is impossible. It was impossible in the Pan Am building. Then we caught a cab and went out to the airport to meet her husband Mike, who was doing some business there, then drove to their home (three hours) in Wilmington, Delaware.

Wednesday 7 February

Wilmington, Delaware. Mike isn't too well. Probably run down, with the strain of the move over. Mike likes it here, although Wilmington is no great shakes, but he is the type of person who could settle anywhere. Pat I think misses the social life a little, and if given the opportunity would catch the next plane back. But she's not unhappy.

Pat drove me around the Dupont Country and although it was early February I should imagine in spring and summer it must be very lovely. I only stayed one night. I caught a train back to New York. Never having been on an American train, I found it most interesting. They seem to be much more quiet than ours. The porter, just before we get into New York, made a speech. 'Ladies and gentlemen, in a few moments we will be in Penn Station New York. Could I please have your tickets and your complaints – I'll take the tickets first.' Then he took our tickets and left, never to be seen again.

Thursday 8 February

Rehearsed most of the day. In the evening, Fred and I went to a place run by an Englishman from Liverpool. All the waiters were English. As a matter of fact, I had a great night there.

Friday 9 February

New York. Just rehearsed today. Spent a lazy day and bought a hat of the Russian type, which is very popular here but will get a laugh at home. But it's so cold here that it's necessary.

Saturday 10 February

New York. Had a band call this morning and rehearsals. Hung about the theatre till Fred came with his nephew. Spent the afternoon with them in a bar on Broadway, telling stories. At five o'clock we came back to the theatre, to get ready for the show. Bing Crosby went on first and kept going wrong. They had to do his bit three times. Even then he sang White Christmas wrong, but they let it go. The show is an Ed Sullivan tribute for Irving Berlin's 80th birthday. We followed Bing Crosby and did our Fred Astaire skit. It was one of the best things we have done here[1]. Bob Hope followed us, and started to do jokes about heart transplants. Not really in good taste, and also had idiot boards all over the front rows. Flew back to England with David Frost, who fell asleep as soon as he sat down. I woke him up about five minutes before landing. He was coming home for three hours, then flying back to New York.

1 Nevertheless, this was Eric and Ernie's last Ed Sullivan show in the States.

Sunday 11 February

Brian met me and took me home. I had lunch at home, and was sat down watching TV in the afternoon. Gail was out riding her horse when at 4.15 Gary runs in to tell me Gail had fallen off her horse and the horse had kicked her in the face, knocking out her tow front teeth. She looked a terrible mess. Joan got the doctor round and got Gail's dentist and had an X-ray. She had one tooth splintered and the other one has been pushed up under her nose and her top jaw had been fractured. She had a lump the size of an egg on her head. She couldn't talk. She looked one hell of a mess. It was arranged for her to go to hospital as soon as the swelling went down, which when you looked at her, you thought it never would. What a black Sunday it's been.

Chapter 15

THE DIARIES 1969

Wednesday 1 January

Weather – snow, freezing. Welcome to 1969. It's exactly eight weeks tomorrow since I had my heart attack[1]. Yesterday I went with my doctor Mike Price to Watford driving golf range for my first real exercise since the attack. I played sixty balls – about one hour. Today I feel stiff, but it's muscles and I feel fine. I've just walked back from Harpenden, approx two miles, with Gary. Joan, Gail, Mum and Dad have gone to Finchley to see Joan's grandmother. She's 86, and she's not too well. I hope she gets well soon as she is a wonderful old lady, but I fear she is failing.

Ernie rang today. He must be bored. Today Lew Grade became Sir Lew! Well, I would have put my money on Bernie Delfont – probably next year. I asked Ernie to send Lew a telegram. I asked Ernie to do it as I didn't trust myself. I would have tried to send a funny one, but knowing Lew's lack of humour I didn't! Knowing Ernie, it will be a short congratulation, probably with a Happy New Year included. Gail has now got a boyfriend, a nice young man called Dick Cave. He plays the piano. This makes Gail practice, and she is now improving.

1 For a detailed account of Eric's first heart attack, see Chapter Seven.

Thursday 2 January

Weather – thawing quite quickly. Well, today was one of the best days since the heart attack. First of all I drove the car to Coldecote Farm at Bushey, taking Gail to see Melody, her horse. She had a good ride. Father came with me in the car. It's the first time I have driven and I really enjoyed it. This afternoon I took Joan to Harpenden, shopping.

Jack Ashworth (auditor) came down from Kendal to see us and will stay with us for a few days. At the moment he is with my father in the lounge playing Putting For Pennies. Father is dead keen and at seventy one has eyes like a hawk. By the sighs and sounds coming from Jack Ashworth and father, the old man is winning. Mike Price brought over George Apthorpe this evening to give me a cardiograph. They are both very pleased with the results, and say the improvement is very good. Soon I should be able to go fishing. I've finished doing my football pools. I must say I really enjoy doing them, and Saturday is a great day when you check them.

Friday 3 January

Weather – snow now gone, very misty, turning to fog. No real excitement today! Got up at eleven this morning – Jack and Joan are talking income tax. They try to keep it away from me. I'm sure they think it will give me another attack. Had a very light lunch – nothing! Gail has gone to ride the horse again, and Joan has just come back with her. Father and I went for a walk round the back of the golf links. Jack has gone to the boat show in town and expects to be back at about nine this evening, but with the weather getting worse it could be much later. Gail and Dick are going over to Finchley for the night, but they don't seem to worry about fog. It must be as you get older you worry more for others. Went to bed early – didn't feel too good.

Saturday 4 January

Weather – very nice sunny morning, turning to fog. Got up this morning and saw Mum, Dad and Jack off. They left for Morecambe at ten o'clock. Had a light breakfast and now going slowly back on to the diet, as I have put on about six or seven pounds over this Christmas and New Year. Joan and I went shopping in Harpenden. Joan drove my car as I was still feeing a bit down. Went to the dentist, and had a filling. Joan waited for me in the waiting room, in case I didn't feel too good, but I was fine. We went shopping, and it's wonderful the way people ask how I feel. Strangers come up and ask me how I feel, and always say, 'Take it easy. Nice to see you again.' I watched our Morecambe & Wise show tonight, and thought it was very good. Gail and Dick have gone out to another party. It must be great to be young. Luton lost in an FA Cup match against Man City – one nil, and that was a penalty. No luck with the football pools. However you can't win them all.

Sunday 5 January

Weather – bright morning. Afternoon and evening – damp and slightly misty. Both Joan and I had a lie in the morning – eleven o'clock, which for Joan makes a pleasant change. I came to bed last night at midnight. Joan waited up for Gail, so she came to bed at 2am. The swimming pool isn't working right. We must have lost about two feet of water in about four days. It's very worrying. They know all about it and they are going to send a frogman. Gary hopes that he will still be on holiday. It's been a very quiet day, very nice, and I've rested today. No walking. I feel very well. I hope it lasts. Anyway, I'm now watching an old terror film on TV. Oh dear, it was made a hundred years ago. It's so old a car drives in central London and parks.

Monday 6 January

Weather – dirty, cold, miserable. Had a letter of thanks from Sir Lew Grade. I'll drop him a line again. Cliff Owen[1] who directed our last two films rang up to find out how I was feeling! He said we should make another film together. I would love to do another film but I don't think it should be with Cliff. Our Christmas show and series seem to be going down very well.

1 Cliff Owen directed Eric and Ernie's second and third feature films, That Riviera Touch and The Magnificent Two. He never

made another film with Eric and Ernie, and Eric and Ernie never starred in another film – not on the big screen, at least. Owen, on the other hand, went on to direct Steptoe & Son, No Sex Please: We're British and The Bawdy Adventures of Tom Jones.

Friday 10 January

Weather – damp. Did nothing really. Hung about the house. Didn't go out anywhere. Nothing type day, but I was glad I was about to see it.

Saturday 11 January

Got up this morning and rang Luton Football Club to fix seats as this is my first visit for a few months. The kick off was at three. Gary was ready at one thirty with his coat on, but the fog was so thick I didn't think they would play. Rang up at two thirty and they had cancelled the match. Gary had to take his coat off – a great pity for both of us[1].

1 Eric and Gary could just as easily have ended up supporting Watford. It just so happened that when Eric decided to take Gary to his first football match, Luton Town were at home that Saturday and Watford were away. However Eric proved to be an invaluable fan, serving as a vice president and director, promoting the club tirelessly on the show, and presiding over the Hatters' dizzy rise from the Third Division to the upper echelons of Division One.

Monday 13 January

Weather – rain. Had a day indoors – nothing much. In the evening we all went to the local cinema to see Tommy Steele[1] in Half A Sixpence. I quite enjoyed it. Tommy has a very pleasant personality. It was a strange feeling to watch the film and think back that while he was making it I had lunch with him at the studios in Borehamwood. At that time Ernie and I were making our TV series for the States. I think I would like to start work soon, but something easy. I'd love to do another film. I get a little worried sometimes as to whether I'm doing the right thing having all this time off, but the doctors say so. I don't want to go back to soon and have another attack. Ernie must be very bored. Gary goes back to school tomorrow. He's had his big bath tonight. He's so clean tonight he looks like a different boy.

1 Tommy Steele, born Thomas Hicks in 1936, was Britain's first rock and roll teen idol. He had a number one hit with Singing The Blues, but his singing was eventually eclipsed by his acting. Before making the movie of Half A Sixpence (based on HG Wells' novel, Kipps) he starred in the stage show of this musical in London's West End and on Broadway.

Tuesday 14 January

Weather – cloudy, rain. The frogman came this morning to see to the pool. It's funny to look out of your window and see a frogman walking about your garden, dressed in flippers and the full bit, even tanks on his back. He was going to Reginald Maudling's[1] place after us. They all seem to have trouble – probably Maudling wants his made deeper to drop Wilson[2] in. Took the Jensen for a warm up drive to St Albans – it goes like a bird, but the rust is starting to show through on the chrome. I must try and keep my writing neater. As a matter of fact, I write too quickly, spell too badly, think too slowly.

Wednesday 15 January

Weather very nice – evening rain. This afternoon Gary, Joan and I went to Finchley to see Joan's family. Polly, Joan's grandmother, was poorly in bed. She looked very ill. Even though she's 87, and has had a great life, it's very sad to see her lying in bed. This evening Gary went back to school. I don't think he was looking forward to it too much. I think he would like the holidays to be schooldays and schooldays to be the holidays. Later this evening I put some sound onto a football film of the Man United v Benfica Cup Final, which I bought. It's great really, because I was at Wembley for that particular match. Man United won 4 – 1. Tonight on BBC England played Romania – one one. It looked a poor game. Tomorrow I go to London for the first time.

Thursday 16 January

Weather – fine and sunny. Joan and I went to London by train. It was a most enjoyable day. First I went to see my dentist, Mr Cross, in Harley Street. This man is a giant. He must be six foot six. He is one of the biggest men I have ever seen. Next to him I feel like Jimmy Clitheroe[1] must feel next to me. After the dentist we called at the office to take Billy Marsh and Mike Grade out for lunch. It was the first time I had seen anyone from the office since the attack. We had a very nice lunch and I must say a lot of laughs, mostly about Leslie, Lew and Bernie[2]. Mike tells some wonderful stories about them. I haven't laughed so much for a long time – so much so my cheeks ached. But what a knockout day it was. I felt fine. One disappointment – I forgot to post the football pools, so I have had to tear them up without looking. It would be terrible if I'd kept them and won. Now I won't know.

1 Jimmy Clitheroe, a midget with a shrill falsetto, was only four foot three. He specialised in playing naughty schoolboys, most notably in the radio show, The Clitheroe Kid.

2 Leslie Grade was Michael Grade's father. Lew Grade and Bernard Delfont were his uncles.

Sunday 19 January

Weather – no wind, overcast, dry. Good fishing day. Gary came home from school for the day today. He really loves home. Harry Worth[1] rang this afternoon, out of the blue. It's funny really. When most people ring me who haven't rung since before the illness, which is now eleven weeks ago, they seem to talk to me very quietly, as if I'm still in bed with a dozen doctors around me. Anyway, Harry rang and asked if he could come over to see me. I was very happy to say yes, as people from showbiz at the moment are a rarity. He came with his 16mm sound projector, to see some of our early shows, which Lew Grade gave to Ernie and I as a present. It was great to see them again, the best thing being that the comedy we did five or six years ago hasn't dated. Harry called them classics, which is high praise indeed. We then fixed up for next Sunday at his place to see some more of ours, and some of his old TV films, which I shall say are minor classics – all in all, a good day.

1 Harry Worth was a Yorkshire comic, a ventriloquist turned stand up. He toured with Eric's heroes, Laurel & Hardy, before winning huge popular acclaim in the BBC sitcom, Here's Harry.

Monday 20 January

Weather – fair. Doc Price came to see me, and it's now got to the stage where I've got to force him to take my pulse, let along examine me. He rather shook me by saying I could (if I wanted, and the way things are going) start work in about three or four weeks – strange thought.

Tuesday 21 January

Weather – overcast, warmish. Doc Price rang up to day to see if I would play a few holes with him this afternoon, so we played six. I was terrible, but no trouble health wise. I feel great for it. He said I should take more exercise now, and next time I should play twelve holes.

Johnny Ammonds, our BBC TV producer, rang – and after asking if I was all right, asked if I could do a TV bit for one of our own programmes, as the BBC want to do a Best of Morecambe & Wise. I jumped at the idea, so I should be back on TV by late February. I'm looking forward to that. It will not be hard. It will only be a small compering bit for one of our own shows, sat down – if I wish. Great – this is the best way to creep in, or back.

Saturday 25 January

Weather – fine then dull. This afternoon I went to see Luton play football. Luton 1, Walsall 0, but it was a poor game. Everybody was so kind, and in the boardroom people came up and asked how I felt. One lady came up and started to talk to me about heart attacks. Her father had three, her husband had four. I think she was quite pleased. But it got them both in the end. I had to laugh.

Appendix 1

One Liners

'I've been watching so many cowboy films lately, I've got saddle bags under my eyes.'

'She's one of those goody goody girls. Every time you turn off the lights, she says, "Goody, goody!"'

'I took her to a posh restaurant, and just to impress her, I ordered the whole meal in French. The waiter was surprised. It was a Chinese restaurant.'

'Some men like girls who come up to their shoulders. Some men like girls who come up to their chin. I like girls who come up to my flat.'

'She tried to conceal her height with subtle disguises, like wearing flat heels or walking on her knees.'

'My wife is the most wonderful woman in the world. And that's not just my opinion – it's hers, too.'

'She was going out of her mind, and her mind was glad she was leaving.'

'I used to dance with Fred Astaire, but really it's much more fun with girls.'

ERIC She was a lovely girl. I was going to marry her and live in the country, and maybe have a couple of kids.

ERNIE Why didn't you?

ERIC She didn't like me.

'Remember, when a girl puts on a swim suit, she may never go near the water – but when she puts on a wedding dress, she means business.'

'She has everything a real he man would want – big muscles and a beard.'

'She looked at me and dropped her lashes. It took us two hours to find them again.'

ERNIE Was she pretty?

ERIC Pretty? You can tell how pretty she was. Her face was her fortune, and she owed her mother money.

'She was married in her grandmother's wedding dress. She looked lovely, but her grandmother looked cold.'

'Then came the wedding. She was so fat, we had to walk down the aisle in single file.'

'I've got the most beautiful wife in the world. There's only one trouble. Her husband wants her back.'

'My wife dresses to kill and cooks the same way.'

'All she asks for is money, money, money. I don't know what she does with it I never give her any.'

'Remember the old saying – hair today, bald tomorrow.'

'I never expect to find the perfect woman, but it's lots of fun looking.'

'What's the use of working? If your ship does come in, you'll find all of your relatives standing on the dock.'

'Tears are what women shed for a fur coat when they're too old to shed anything else.'

'People are funny – it takes them years to teach a child to talk. Then they tell him to keep quiet.'

'You are now looking at the man who owns hell. My wife gave it to me this morning.'

'She washed my shirts this morning and they came out beautiful and white – even the blue ones.'

'She said, "Would you like to see me in something flowing?" I said, "Yes – the River Thames."'

'It's easier for a woman to get a seat in parliament than on a bus.'

'Never run after a bus or a woman. There'll be another along in a minute. Maybe there aren't so many after midnight, but the ones you get are faster.'

'Eat, drink and be merry, for tomorrow you may not be able to afford it.'

'They say bread cast upon the water comes back to you a hundred fold. Fine! But what am I going to do with a hundred wet loaves?'

'I remember my first fight. I remember my last fight. Same fight.'

'In the first round I had him worried. He thought he'd killed me.'

'A clock that's stopped is right twice a day.'

'Conscience doesn't keep you from doing anything wrong. It just keeps you from enjoying it.'

'Conversation – when three women are talking. Gossip – when one of them leaves.'

'The average man could be replaced by a hot water bottle.'

'You can imagine how hot it was – an Englishman had his overcoat unbuttoned.'

'My wardrobe is closed when I fasten my jacket.'

'I often wonder if an infant has more fun in infancy than an adult has in adultery?'

'At least there's one good thing about hell – nobody can tell you where to go.'

'They say clever men make the best husbands. Clever men don't become husbands.'

'Don't ever question your wife's judgement. Look at who she married.'

'There is only one thing better than chasing women – catching them.'

'Caterpillar – an upholstered worm.'

'Out of bounds – a tired kangaroo.'

'Agent – a man who's annoyed because you get 90% of his salary.'

'Blueprint – a French postcard.'

'Perpetual Motion – a cow drinking a pail of milk.'

'Widow – a woman who always knows where her husband is.'

ERIC Are you going to apologise?

ERNIE Me? Apologise?

ERIC Thank you, you're very kind.

'Virus – what people who can't spell pneumonia get.'

'People pay good money to read words they would slap their children for saying.'

ERNIE Are you an early riser?

ERIC That depends who I'm with.

ERIC I used to be an alcoholic but I'm almost cured.

ERNIE Almost cured?

ERIC Yes, I'm only a drunk now.

ERNIE You say you've been married twice?

ERIC Yes.

ERNIE And where are you wives now?

ERIC One's dead, and one's living in Gateshead – so she might as well be.

'Henry Cooper is a pugilist but who's got the nerve to tell him?

'He who laughs last plays for Luton'

'It's better to have halitosis than no breath at all.'

'At the end of the diet I weighted nine stone twelve, including the wheel-chair.'

'She's had her face lifted so many times, the dimple on her chin is really her navel.'

'I could run the hundred yards dash in seven seconds – I knew a short cut.'

'Poor? I couldn't afford the doctor's bill. You're looking at the only man in the world who's had his appendix taken out and put back in again.'

'Mustard bath – that's the best thing in the world. Let's face it – you never see a ham sandwich with a cold.'

'If you were to put all the arteries and veins and capillaries out end to end, that man would probably die.'

'Medical books claim that there are over 400 sexual positions, but they never say where to apply for them.'

'This doctor has a great reputation. They say if you're at death's door, he'll pull you through.'

'I walked into the surgery, the first thing the doctor did was remove the swelling from my wallet.'

'I'm so full of penicillin at the moment, every time I sneeze I cure somebody.'

'What a detective! Once a burglar robbed a safe wearing calf skin gloves. He took the fingerprints and five days later he arrested a cow in Surrey.'

'My mother in law can't be with me today. She's coming along later on, on the four o'clock broom.'

'The man who said "All men are created equal" has never been in a footballer's changing room.'

'Never play ping pong with your mouth open.'

'He has a very athletic figure – he's shaped just like a hockey stick.'

'I used to play football in my youth. Then my eyes went bad. That's why I became a referee.'

'Boxing gloves always cramp my style. I mean, how can you pull hair with boxing gloves on?'

I believe in honesty. I once found a wallet with three hundred pounds in it. Did I keep it? I did not. I went right out and put an ad in the lost and found column of the Budapest Daily News.'

ERNIE I think I shall sit down.

ERIC I thought you were sat down.

'Seventy one per cent of the world is covered by water. The other twenty nine per cent is covered by mortgages.'

'I was never carried out of the ring on a stretcher. I had silver handles sewn onto my shorts.'

'My eyes are no good anymore – I've got my wife to prove it.'

'The fisherman was telling me lies. He told me the fish were biting. If they were, they were biting each other.'

'I hit him with a chicken and he yelled, "Foul!"'

'I went to a football match. Next to me, there was a woman shouting, "Kill the ref! Kill the ref!" It was the ref's wife.'

'This is an expensive cigar I'm smoking. I know it's expensive. It was thrown out of a Rolls.'

'The last time I was as nervous as this was when I was trapped in a lift with Larry Grayson.'

'I didn't come here to be insulted. I could have stayed at home and read my fan mail.'

'After every joke I got a tremendous round of applause. Then I found out there was a waiter trying to get some HP Sauce out of a bottle.'

'They've got a machine now that handles a million words a minute. It's called an electronic mother in law.'

'There's only one trouble with being best man at a wedding. You never get a chance to prove it.'

'Don't talk to me about Luton Town Football Club. We now do a lap of honour when we get a corner.'

'Our horse was so old, we had to dunk his hay for him.'

'I've never seen such a hairy chest. He wasn't born – he was trapped.'

ERNIE Have you got the maracas?
ERIC No, it's the way I walk.

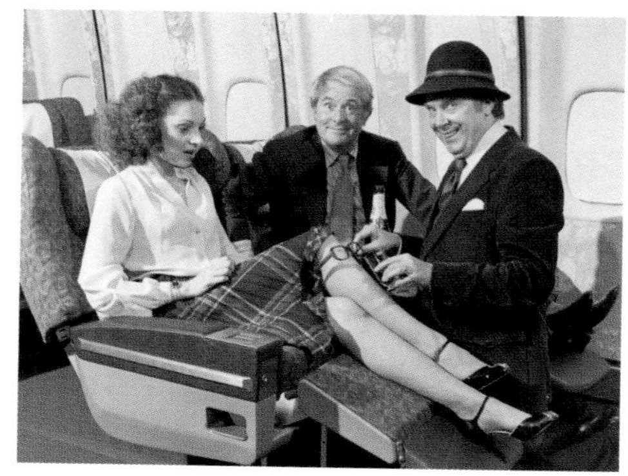

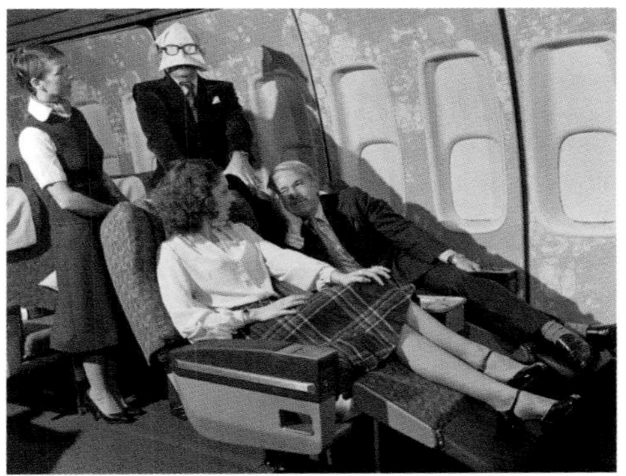

'They're making fantastic strides in the world of genetics. They've now crossed an octopus with a mink. I've got a fur coat with eight sleeves.'

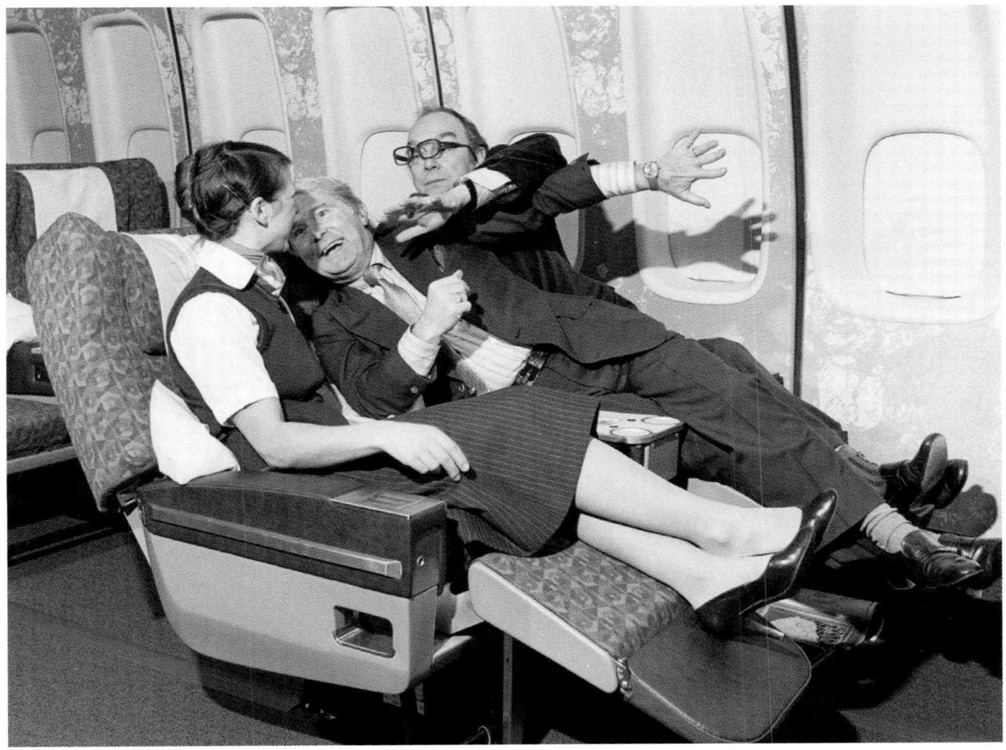

ERNIE You're thinking about something, aren't you?

ERIC Yes.

ERNIE What?

ERIC How to dispose of your body.

Appendix 2

ERIC'S NOTEBOOKS

DICK TURPIN

SHE'S NUDE... HAS HER BACK TO ME... LOOKS LIKE KOJAK WITH A DEEP FROWN....

—

LARGE PHOTO (LIFE SIZE). UP AGAINST ROCK. AS COACH GOES BY IT HAS TO GIVE THE IDEA OF FLATTENING ME AGAINST THE ROCK... PICTURE THEN SLIDES DOWN ROCK.

—

COACH GOES OVER MY FOOT ON ONE HOLD UP... COACHMAN IGNORES HOLDUP COMPLETELY... WITH SHOUTS OF PARDON -- SPEAK UP!! (STAND AND DELIVER). LOUDER. SPEAK LOUDER...
COACH GOES BY. INTO PUDDLE... MUD ALL OVER FACE. OUT AS IN ADVERT FOR MAN. CIGARS...

—

IN BAR WITH TWO BUSTY GIRLS ONE EITHER SIDE... SOMEONE RUSHES IN AND SAYS WHICH ONE'S DICK!

—

GIRL. 'DON'T YOU KNOW WHAT GOOD CLEAN FUN IS.
ERIC ... NO WHAT GOOD IS IT.

—

GIRL. 'WHAT DO YOU THINK OF THIS (LACE ETC.)
IT'S DONE SO [illegible]
ERIC. REALLY! DID YOU WEAVE IT YOURSELF.

GIRL. ONLY ONE MAN HAS EVER KISSED ME - MY HUSBAND.
ERIC. ARE YOU BRAGGING OR COMPLAINING

GIRL. STAY HERE. I HAVE TO FIX MY FACE
ERIC. YOU'LL FIND SOME PUTTY IN THE KITCHEN.

AND ALL THE LADIES WHO [illegible]
HAVE TO [illegible]
[illegible] YOU [illegible]
NO PHONE NUMBER

X QUICKIE
DON JUAN — CLIMBING
UP TO BALCONY — B.FUL GIRL
ON BAL. (MUSIC)
DON. KATHRINE. (BREATHLESS
KAT. DON ~~JUAN~~.. PASSION)
D. JUAN PICKS UP K. AND
DROPS HER OVER BALCONY
(KILL DON JUAN.)
BREAK FLYNN
FIRST REEL

XMAS 76

JUST A MOMENT. I'M GETTING ABOUT AS MUCH ATTENTION AS A ? AT A NUDIST CAMP.

—

MATA HARI. ERIC. YOU LOOK TIRED.
I'M ALL IN.
YOU DON'T LOOK IT.

—

SHE WAS A STRIPPER. — HER RIGHT HAND DIDN'T KNOW WHAT HER LEFT HAND WAS UNDOING

—

SHE WAS A BAD DRESSER. SHE WALKED LIKE A [illegible] WASHING MACHINE.

—

[illegible]
[illegible]
I'D LIKE TO WATCH MY [illegible].

ERIKA. SOMEONE IN HOLLYWOOD WITH A FIGURE LIKE YOURS.
[illegible].
HE'S NOT HAPPY ABOUT IT TOO.

FROM SO POOR. MY MOTHER FATHER COULDN'T AFFORD A LARGE FAMILY - 2 OF MY BROTHERS ARE RENTED.

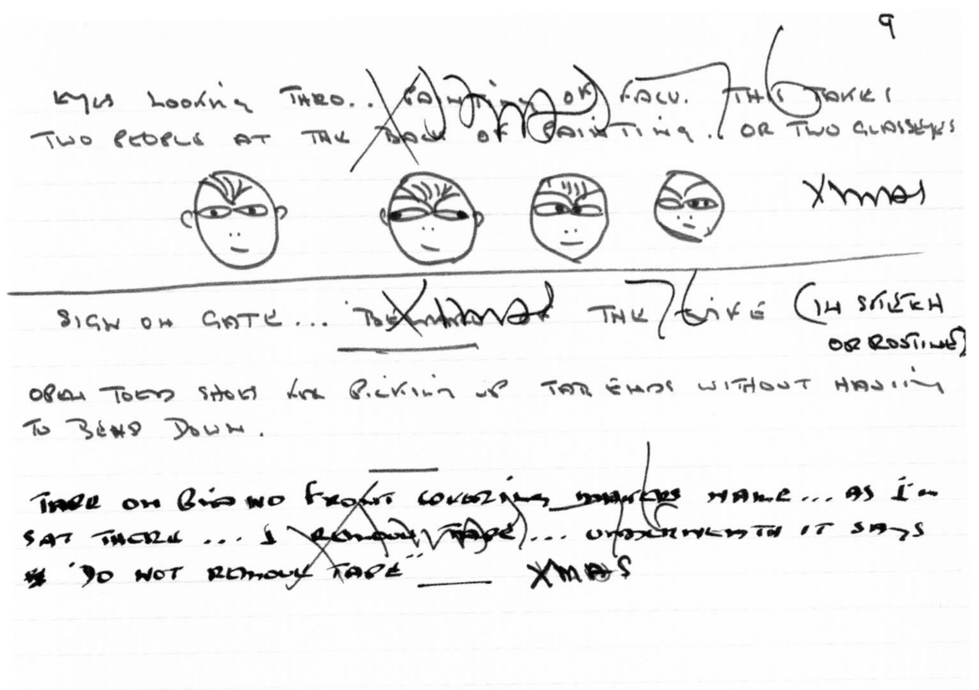

I

T.V. ROMP IDEAS

I GULLIVERS TRAV. 2 MOTOR RACING....

3. FU MANCHU MEETS DRACULA..

4 FLASH GORDON.. EMPRO. MING..
TRAP SEQUENCE – PANTO. MAY HAVE TO BE DONE
IN THEATRE. (THREE CAMERA)

DICK TURPINS RIDE TO YORK (DONE)

HOLDING UP THE STAGE COACH
AND HAVING THE MUD IN THE FACE
AND MUSIC OF AIR ON G STRING
(AD FOR CIGAR): "NEVER MET A
MAN FROM YORRKK.......

CAPTAIN BLOODLESS

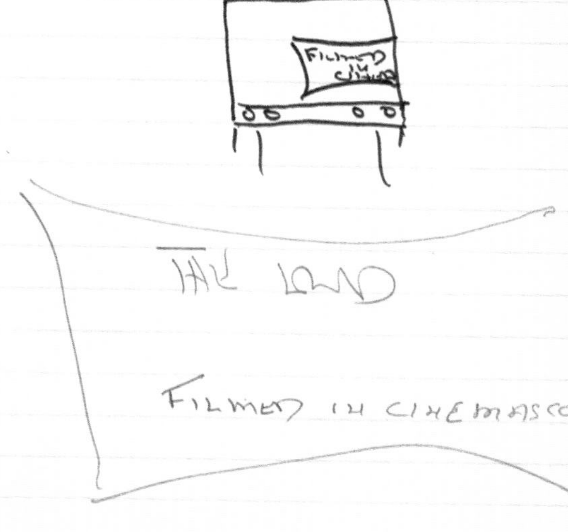

I DIDN'T KNOW WHETHER TO PUT MY HANDS UP AND FIGHT LIKE A MAN OR PUT MY HANDS UP AND RUN LIKE A RABBIT.

ERIC HERE'S YOUR SCRIPT. WAIT A MINUTE I'LL GET SOMEONE TO READ IT FOR YOU

MY NAME IS A HOUSEHOLD WORD. THE ONLY TROUBLE IS — YOU CAN'T SAY IT IN FRONT OF CHILDREN

BUY UP BIG BLACK HAT WITH BLACK PLUME IN IT... ON ELASTIC. WHEN YOU PULL IT DOWN TO YOUR CHIN IT LOOKS LIKE A BEARD MUST BE STRONG AND COME QUICKLY.

WHITY BEARD
ON ROUTE.
DRINKING IN PUB.

ALSO GLASSES
UP AND DOWN

16

CHARLIE II XMAS

YOU ARE LOOKING AT THE GREATEST SINGLE ARGUMENT FOR TWIN BEDS.

HE CAN'T HELP IT. HE COMES FROM A LONG LINE HIS MOTHER SHOULDN'T HAVE LISTENED TO.

IF SOMEONE DESCRIBED HIM TO YOU AND I DIDN'T KNOW YOU. I WOULDN'T BELIEVE HIM.

LOOK: HE MAY ACT LIKE AN IDIOT HE MAY TALK LIKE AN IDIOT. BUT PLEASE DON'T LET

3

MUSICAL NUMBERS.

SINGING IN THE RAIN. ERNIE AS GENE KELLY. DONE AS NEAR AS POSSIBLE: ERIC AS POLICEMAN UNDER WATER PIPE.. EVERYTHING ON SET INCLUDING ERN STAYS DRY.. ONLY WATER IS FROM DRAIN PIPES. TWO DRAIN PIPES AS ERIC MOVES FROM WORKING ONE TO THE OTHER DRY ONE WATER STOPS IN FIRST ONE AND STARTS AGAIN IN SECOND AND VICA VERSA.... TWO CLOSE UPS OF ERIC AND TWO CERTAIN POINTS IN MUSIC. THE REST IS SHOT LONG. NO CLOSE OR MID SHOTS WHILE NUMBER STARTS.. ERNIE AT THE END OF SONG GIVES ERIC THE UMBRELLA! ERIC PUTS UMBRELLA UP AND UMBRELLA FLAPS STAY DOWN BUT SPOKES GO UP FADE OUT.....

XMAS – 76

BIG SPENDER. EXACTLY THE SAME AS FILM WITH ERN & I AS TWO OF THE GIRLS...... SAME SHOOTING ROUTINE....

DONE

CHATTANOOGA CHOO CHOO. GLEN MILLER ARR. ERN AND SELF PLAY ALL PARTS...... SEPERATLY & TOGETHER. EACH PART IS RULED BY THE WORDS OF THE MUSIC.... THIS WILL BE HARD TO DO AS IT WILL MEAN MANY STOPS & STARTS. (AWAY DAY).

SHOW ME THE WAY TO GO HOME: TOP HAT & TAILS. DONE

SLAUGHTER ON 10th AVE. DONE

THREE HANDED "SIDE BY SIDE" SAME ARRANG. AS WE GOT US" SIDE ... MAGIC GOEMEY. MAYBE ARTHUR AS STATUE IN PARK PLAYS MOUTH ORGAN. COMPLETELY WHITE.

XMAS – 76

7

PROP IDEAS

PERSON SAT DOWN READING MAG. HOLDING MAG CLOSE TO FACE UP TO JUST BELOW EYES. PICTURE ON MAG. IS HALF A FACE...

GROUP OF SINGERS (CHOIR ~~AT XMAS SHOW~~) AS THEY REACH A HIGH NOTE ONE OF THEM RISES INTO AIR...

KEN + I HIDDEN IN CHOIR....

COULD BE COLD OPENING FOR XMAS SHOW. KEN + I GO UP ON LAST HIGH NOTE.....

ARMS GETTING LONGER THRO SONG. (GOODIES DID SOMETHIN SIMILAR)

GIRL SINGS SONG. 'IF I HAD A TALKING PICTURE OF YOU' LINE IN SONG SAYS 'WHAT DO YOU THINK OF IT SO FAR? PICTURE (ME) MOUTH MOVES. 'RUBBISH'

ERIC + KEN. AS TWO ~~CHIPS ON A~~ PLATE. SALT.... VINEGAR SAUCE. BIG FORK .. KNIFE ... XMAS

PIANO (GRAND)). OPERA SINGER... SINGER SINGS FIRST NOTE... VERY LOUD... AS SHE '''HITS''' FIRST NOTE. PIANO COLLAPSES ... MANY LOOKS... !!! DONE

T.V. FACING CAMERA... (FACE) L + G. IT THE DES O'CONNER ~~SHOW~~ THEATRE CURTAINS CLOSE OVER T.V. SCREEN...
XMAS

LINES

MEDICAL..... THIS GIRL HAD EVERYTHING ... THEY QUARANTINED HER THIS MORNING ..

.

THEY GIVE YOU A PEP PILL AND A TRANQUILLIZER PILL ... THE IDEA BEING .. YOU GET THIS TREMENDOUS URGE TO MAKE LOVE TO A WOMAN .. BUT IF YOU CANT FIND ONE ... IT DOESNT MATTER ......

.

THEY HAVE MADE FANTASTIC STRIDES IN THE WORLD OF GENETICS ... THEY HAVE NOW CROSSED AN OCTIPUS WITH A MINK.... GOT A FUR COAT WITH EIGHT SLEEVES

.

ITS BETTER TO HAVE HILOTOSIS THAN NO BREATH AT ALL...

.

RECENT SURV. SHOWS THAT OUT OF 601 DOCTORS ... 302 WERE ...

.

I FINALLY GOT A DOCTOR TO TREAT ME .... I WAS THRILLED ... BECAUSE ALL THE OTHER DOCTORS WANTED MONEY....

.

HE SAID HE'D EXAMINE ME FOR A LIVER.... I TOLD HIM ..IF HE FOUND IT I'D SPLIT IT WITH HIM....

.

FOR YEARS I'VE BEEN STONE DEAF ... BUT AFTER DRINKING ONLY ONE BOTTLE OF YOUR PRODUCT.. I HEARD FROM MY SISTER IN IPSWICH

WALKS TO THEM [redacted] (CAMERA DOES NOT FOLLOW HIM SO THE THREE FIGURES ARE FULL LENGTH IN BACKGROUND YOU HEAR NO REAL WORDS JUST NOISE AND ODD WORDS LIKE OH YEAH ... WHO IS .. DON'T YOU DARE — ERIC JOINS THEM AND GETS PUSHED HE NOW PUSHES BACK AND SOON ALL THREE ARE PUSHING AND SHOUTING THE FIGHT GETS BIGGER AND BIGGER ... ENDING UP ON THE FLOOR)... FADE ..... AFTER NEXT SPOT CAMERA SHOW THEM STILL ROLLING ABOUT ON THE FLOOR. AFTER EACH SPOT OR TWO ... IT COMES BACK TO THEM. THEIR CLOTHES BECOME TORN AND THEIR HAIR DISHEVELLED ETC ETC. —

INTRO. TO FRANK SINATRA.... AS ERN & I INTRO. HIM. YOU SEE CURTAIN MOVE .. AND WALKS C STAGE — ANY WAY ERN & I WALK BACKWARDS OFF STAGE HOLDING ARMS OUT TO FRANK. — CAMERA FOLLOWS ERN & I .... SIDE OF STAGE CAMERA IS STILL ON ERN & I ... WE HEAR SINATRA SINGING (RECORD) LOUD. COMING WELL .. ERN & I LOOKING AT HIM ON STAGE. SAY. 'GREAT.. FANCY HIM DOING OUR SHOW. WHAT A GREAT PERFORMER. ECT: ERN AND I GO OUT TO HIM ~~AT THE END~~ OF HIS SONG BUT. VIEWER ONLY SEES LEGS OF SINATRA GOING BACK THRO CURTAIN: AND. NOW CHEERING LIKE MAD .... ERIC & ERN TRYING TO GET HIM TO COME OUT THRO THE CURTAINS

Appendix 3

Notes

HARPENDEN

1 Memories of Eric by Gary Morecambe & Martin Sterling (Andre Deutsch, 1999)

2 Stella by Eric Morecambe with Gary Morecambe (Severn House, 1986)

3 Eric wore this outfit to sing his comic song, 'I'm Not All There', which he inherited from the male impersonator, Ella Shields. However even at such an early age, this wasn't his only costume. For other turns, he'd wear an old straw hat and a moth eaten fur coat – a get up popularised by Bud 'Underneath The Arches' Flanagan.

MORECAMBE

1 Eric & Ernie – The Autobiography of Morecambe & Wise with Dennis Holman (WH Allen, 1973)

2 Eric & Ernie – The Autobiography of Morecambe & Wise with Dennis Holman (WH Allen, 1973)

3 Eric & Ernie – The Autobiography of Morecambe & Wise with Dennis Holman (WH Allen, 1973)

4 Eric & Ernie – The Autobiography of Morecambe & Wise with Dennis Holman (WH Allen, 1973)

5 Morecambe & Wise – Behind The Sunshine by Gary Morecambe & Martin Sterling (Robson Books, 1994)

6 Sunday Times, 16 December 1979

7 Morecambe & Wise – Behind The Sunshine by Gary Morecambe & Martin Sterling (Robson Books, 1994)

BARTHOLOMEW & WISEMAN

1 Morecambe & Wise – You Can't See The Join by Jeremy Novick (Chameleon, 1997)

2 Daily Express, 7 January 1939

3 Eric & Ernie – The Autobiography of Morecambe & Wise with Dennis Holman (WH Allen, 1973)

4 Still On My Way To Hollywood by Ernie Wise with Trevor Barnes (Duckworth, 1990)

5 Eric & Ernie – The Autobiography of Morecambe & Wise with Dennis Holman (WH Allen, 1973)

6 Eric & Ernie – The Autobiography of Morecambe & Wise with Dennis Holman (WH Allen, 1973)

MORECAMBE & WISE

1 Eric & Ernie – The Autobiography of Morecambe & Wise with Dennis Holman (WH Allen, 1973)

2 Eric & Ernie – The Autobiography of Morecambe & Wise with Dennis Holman (WH Allen, 1973)

3 Named after Ernest Bevin (1881–1951), the eminent trade unionist and Labour politician, who mobilised the British workforce during World War Two as Churchill's Minister of Labour & National Service.

4 Eric & Ernie – The Autobiography of Morecambe & Wise with Dennis Holman (WH Allen, 1973)

5 Morecambe & Wise – You Can't See The Join by Jeremy Novick (Chameleon, 1997)

6 Eric & Ernie – The Autobiography of Morecambe & Wise with Dennis Holman (WH Allen, 1973)

7 Eric did make a few solo appearances in his later years, including a couple of short films for Anglia TV, based on poems by poet laureate Sir John Betjamen, but by and large, from this day on, he did virtually no high profile work without Ernie.

8 Morecambe & Wise On Stage (Thames) 17 February 1987

9 Eric & Ernie – The Autobiography of Morecambe & Wise with Dennis Holman (WH Allen, 1973)

10 The Straight Man – My Life In Comedy by Nicholas Parsons (Weidenfeld & Nicolson, 1994)

THE VARIETY YEARS

1 Eric & Ernie – The Autobiography of Morecambe & Wise with Dennis Holman (WH Allen, 1973)

2 Eric & Ernie – The Autobiography of Morecambe & Wise with Dennis Holman (WH Allen, 1973)

3 Funny Man – Eric Morecambe by Gary Morecambe (Methuen, 1982)

4 Morecambe & Wife by Joan Morecambe with Michael Leitch (Pelham, 1985)

5 The People, 25 April 1954

6 Eric & Ernie – The Autobiography of Morecambe & Wise with Dennis Holman (WH Allen, 1973)

7 There's No Answer To That! An Autobiography of Morecambe & Wise with Michael Freedland (Arthur Barker, 1981)

8 Mr Lonely by Eric Morecambe (Eyre Methuen, 1981)

9 Eric & Ernie – The Autobiography of Morecambe & Wise with Dennis Holman (WH Allen, 1973)

THE ATV YEARS

1 Memories of Eric by Gary Morecambe & Martin Sterling (Andre Deutsch, 1999)

2 Memories of Eric by Gary Morecambe & Martin Sterling (Andre Deutsch, 1999)

3 Eric & Ernie – The Autobiography of Morecambe & Wise with Dennis Holman (WH Allen, 1973)

4 Morecambe & Wife by Joan Morecambe with Michael Leitch (Pelham, 1985)

5 Mr Lonely by Eric Morecambe (Eyre Methuen, 1981)

6 New York Daily News Record, 6 May 1968

7 The Times, 25 March 1965

8 Cliff Owen directed Peter Sellers in The Wrong Arm of The Law (1962), another crime caper, also starring Bernard Cribbins, Nanette Newman and John Le Mesurier.

9 There's No Answer To That! An Autobiography of Morecambe & Wise with Michael Freedland (Arthur Barker, 1981)

KEEP GOING YOUR FOOL

1 There's No Answer To That! An Autobiography of Morecambe & Wise with Michael Freedland (Arthur Barker, 1981)
To be fair to Lew Grade, colour transmission on British commercial TV only became feasible in 1968 with the award of the new ITV franchises. BBC2, conversely, had been pioneering colour TV since 1967.

2 Bring Me Sunshine – The Life & Soul of Eric Morecambe, BBC Omnibus, 23 December 1998

3 Bring Me Sunshine – The Life & Soul of Eric Morecambe, BBC Omnibus, 23 December 1998

4 Morecambe & Wise – You Can't See The Join by Jeremy Novick (Chameleon, 1997)

5 Memories of Eric by Gary Morecambe & Martin Sterling (Andre Deutsch, 1999)

6 Morecambe & Wise – You Can't See The Join by Jeremy Novick (Chameleon, 1997)

7 There's No Answer To That! An Autobiography of Morecambe & Wise with Michael Freedland (Arthur Barker, 1981)

8 Memories of Eric by Gary Morecambe & Martin Sterling (Andre Deutsch, 1999)

9 Eric & Ernie – The Autobiography of Morecambe & Wise with Dennis Holman (WH Allen, 1973)

10 Eric & Ernie – The Autobiography of Morecambe & Wise with Dennis Holman (WH Allen, 1973)

11 Morecambe & Wife by Joan Morecambe with Michael Leitch (Pelham, 1985)

12 Morecambe & Wife by Joan Morecambe with Michael Leitch (Pelham, 1985)

13 Eric & Ernie – The Autobiography of Morecambe & Wise with Dennis Holman (WH Allen, 1973)

14 Bring Me Sunshine – The Life & Soul of Eric Morecambe, BBC Omnibus, 23 December 1998

THE BBC YEARS

1 Bring Me Sunshine – The Life & Soul of Eric Morecambe, BBC Omnibus, 23 December 1998

2 Fools Rush In – BBC Omnibus, 18 February 1973

3 Eric & Ernie – The Autobiography of Morecambe & Wise with Dennis Holman (WH Allen, 1973)

4 There's No Answer To That! An Autobiography of Morecambe & Wise with Michael Freedland (Arthur Barker, 1981)

5 Bring Me Sunshine – The Life & Soul of Eric Morecambe, BBC Omnibus, 23 December 1998

6 Memories of Eric by Gary Morecambe & Martin Sterling (Andre Deutsch, 1999)

7 The Illustrated Morecambe by Gary Morecambe (Macdonald, 1986)

8 The Observer, 9 September 1973

9 The Best of Morecambe & Wise by Eddie Braben (Woburn Press, 1974)

10 Daily Express, 22 March 1999

11 The Observer, 9 September 1973

12 There's No Answer To That! An Autobiography of Morecambe & Wise with Michael Freedland (Arthur Barker, 1981)

13 Morecambe & Wise – You Can't See The Join by Jeremy Novick (Chameleon, 1997)

14 There's No Answer To That! An Autobiography of Morecambe & Wise with Michael Freedland (Arthur Barker, 1981)

15 Memories of Eric by Gary Morecambe & Martin Sterling (Andre Deutsch, 1999)

16 Eric Morecambe – Life's Not Hollywood, It's Cricklewood by Gary Morecambe (BBC Books, 2003)

17 There's No Answer To That! An Autobiography of Morecambe & Wise with Michael Freedland (Arthur Barker, 1981)

18 Memories of Eric by Gary Morecambe & Martin Sterling (Andre Deutsch, 1999)

THE ATV YEARS

1 London Evening Standard, 27 January 1978

2 Morecambe & Wise – Behind The Sunshine by Gary Morecambe & Martin Sterling (Robson Books, 1994)

3 Funny Man – Eric Morecambe by Gary Morecambe (Methuen, 1982)

4 Memories of Eric by Gary Morecambe & Martin Sterling (Andre Deutsch, 1999)

5 There's No Answer To That! An Autobiography of Morecambe & Wise with Michael Freedland (Arthur Barker, 1981)

6 Sunday Telegraph, 14 September 1980
7 Morecambe & Wise – You Can't See The Join by Jeremy Novick (Chameleon, 1997)
8 Morecambe & Wife by Joan Morecambe with Michael Leitch (Pelham, 1985)
9 Still On My Way To Hollywood by Ernie Wise with Trevor Barnes (Duckworth, 1990)
10 Morecambe & Wife by Joan Morecambe with Michael Leitch (Pelham, 1985)
11 Bring Me Sunshine – The Life & Soul of Eric Morecambe, BBC Omnibus, 23 December 1998
12 Morecambe & Wise – Behind The Sunshine by Gary Morecambe & Martin Sterling (Robson Books, 1994)
13 Memories of Eric by Gary Morecambe & Martin Sterling (Andre Deutsch, 1999)
14 Euston Films' movies included an Armchair Cinema classic called Regan, about a maverick Flying Squad detective, which inspired the highly successful Thames TV series, The Sweeney (Sweeney Todd – Flying Squad), starring Dennis Waterman as Detective Sergeant Carter and John Thaw as Detective Inspector Regan. The series spawned two more movies, after Eric and Ernie made a guest appearance in the final episode.

BRING ME SUNSHINE

1 Morecambe & Wife by Joan Morecambe with Michael Leitch (Pelham, 1985)
2 The Visitor, Morecambe, 2 February 1977
3 Morecambe & Wise – Behind The Sunshine by Gary Morecambe & Martin Sterling (Robson Books, 1994)
4 The Illustrated Morecambe by Gary Morecambe (Macdonald, 1986)
5 There's No Answer To That! An Autobiography of Morecambe & Wise with Michael Freedland (Arthur Barker, 1981)
6 Morecambe & Wife by Joan Morecambe with Michael Leitch (Pelham, 1985)
7 Morecambe & Wife by Joan Morecambe with Michael Leitch (Pelham, 1985)
8 Bring Me Sunshine – The Life & Soul of Eric Morecambe, BBC Omnibus, 23 December 1998
9 Morecambe & Wife by Joan Morecambe with Michael Leitch (Pelham, 1985)
10 Bring Me Sunshine – The Life & Soul of Eric Morecambe, BBC Omnibus, 23 December 1998
11 Bring Me Sunshine – The Life & Soul of Eric Morecambe, BBC Omnibus, 23 December 1998
12 Bring Me Sunshine – The Life & Soul of Eric Morecambe, BBC Omnibus, 23 December 1998
13 Bring Me Sunshine – The Life & Soul of Eric Morecambe, BBC Omnibus, 23 December 1998
14 Morecambe & Wife by Joan Morecambe with Michael Leitch (Pelham, 1985)
15 Bring Me Sunshine – The Life & Soul of Eric Morecambe, BBC Omnibus, 23 December 1998
16 Bring Me Sunshine – The Life & Soul of Eric Morecambe, BBC Omnibus, 23 December 1998
17 Morecambe & Wise – Behind The Sunshine by Gary Morecambe & Martin Sterling (Robson Books, 1994)
18 Daily Express, 29 May 1984
19 Daily Star, 29 May 1984
20 Morecambe & Wise – Behind The Sunshine by Gary Morecambe & Martin Sterling (Robson Books, 1994)
21 Morecambe & Wise – Behind The Sunshine by Gary Morecambe & Martin Sterling (Robson Books, 1994)
22 Morecambe & Wife by Joan Morecambe with Michael Leitch (Pelham, 1985)
23 The Guardian, 29 May 1984
24 Bring Me Sunshine – The Life & Soul of Eric Morecambe, BBC Omnibus, 23 December 1998

WHAT DO YOU THINK OF IT SO FAR?

1 The Observer, 9 September 1973
2 The Book What I Wrote – Eric, Ernie And Me by Eddie Braben (Hodder & Stoughton, 2004)
3 The Kenneth Williams Diaries edited by Russell Davies (HarperCollins, 1993)
4 Morecambe & Wise – Behind The Sunshine by Gary Morecambe & Martin Sterling (Robson Books, 1994)
5 Eric Morecambe – Life's Not Hollywood, It's Cricklewood by Gary Morecambe (BBC Books, 2003)
Mike & Bernie Winters were a likeable and successful double act. It was simply their misfortune that their career coincided with Eric and Ernie's.
6 Morecambe & Wise – Behind The Sunshine by Gary Morecambe & Martin Sterling (Robson Books, 1994)
7 Morecambe & Wise – Behind The Sunshine by Gary Morecambe & Martin Sterling (Robson Books, 1994)
8 Radio Times, 14 May 1994
9 The Guardian, 24 July 1999
10 Lancashire Evening Post, 23 July 1999
11 The Guardian, 22 March 1999
12 Morecambe & Wise – You Can't See The Join by Jeremy Novick (Chameleon, 1997)
13 TV Times, 19 December 1981
14 Eric Morecambe – Life's Not Hollywood, It's Cricklewood by Gary Morecambe (BBC Books, 2003)
15 The Guardian, 6 November 2001

Appendix 4

BIBLIOGRAPHY

EVERY BIOGRAPHER FOLLOWS in the footsteps of other authors, and I am indebted to the writers of all of the books below. If you've enjoyed this one, do seek them out. You're bound to enjoy them too. Especially enjoyable are Gary Morecambe's affectionate but remarkably objective portraits of his father, and Graham McCann's meticulous study, which looks set to remain the definitive biography for many years to come. Joan Morecambe's Morecambe & Wife is a warm and intimate memoir by a woman who was widowed twenty years ago, but remains very much Mrs Morecambe to this day. Mark Lewisohn's encyclopaedic TV guide is the bible of British humour on the box, for Eric and Ernie, and countless other comics besides. Nick Hern's collection of Kenneth Tynan profiles places Eric alongside great comics such as Lenny Bruce and WC Fields, as well as 'serious' actors like John Gielgud and Laurence Olivier, where he has every right to stand. And finally, Dennis Holman and Michael Freedland have done Eric and Ernie an enormous service by compiling their joint autobiographies, and preserving their memories, in their own words, while they were still alive. Writers who perform this delicate task are often erroneously dismissed as ghostwriters – a term that pays scant credit to their discreet but important role. 'It is doubtful whether much that is memorable will be left in print about him,' wrote Tynan of Eric Morecambe. 'He may well be a literary casualty, because he lacks the easily identifiable characteristics by which other comics impress themselves on the memory.' (1) Tynan was right about most things, but he was wrong about this one. There has already been much that is memorable in print about Eric Morecambe, and my thanks are due to everyone who wrote all these books that came before.

The Best of Morecambe & Wise
by Eddie Braben (Woburn Press, 1974)

The Book What I Wrote – Eric, Ernie And Me
by Eddie Braben (Hodder & Stoughton, 2004)

Funny Way To Be A Hero
by John Fisher (Frederick Muller, 1973)

There's No Answer To That! An Autobiography of Morecambe & Wise
with Michael Freedland (Arthur Barker, 1981)

Eric & Ernie – The Autobiography of Morecambe & Wise
with Dennis Holman (WH Allen, 1973)

The Radio Times Guide To TV Comedy
by Mark Lewisohn (BBC Books, 1998)

Morecambe & Wise
by Graham McCann (Fourth Estate, 1998)

Mr Lonely by Eric Morecambe
(Eyre Methuen, 1981)

The Reluctant Vampire by Eric Morecambe
(Methuen, 1982)

The Vampire's Revenge by Eric Morecambe
(Methuen, 1983)

Stella by Eric Morecambe
with Gary Morecambe (Severn House, 1986)

Funny Man – Eric Morecambe
by Gary Morecambe (Methuen, 1982)

The Illustrated Morecambe
by Gary Morecambe (Macdonald, 1986)

Eric Morecambe – Life's Not Hollywood, It's Cricklewood
by Gary Morecambe (BBC Books, 2003)

Hard Act To Follow – Intimate Stories of Life With Superstar Parents
by Gary Morecambe & Michael Sellers
(Blake Publishing, 1997)

Memories of Eric
by Gary Morecambe & Martin Sterling
(Andre Deutsch, 1999)

Morecambe & Wise – Behind The Sunshine
by Gary Morecambe & Martin Sterling
(Robson Books, 1994)

Morecambe & Wife
by Joan Morecambe with Michael Leitch
(Pelham, 1985)

Morecambe & Wise – You Can't See The Join
by Jeremy Novick (Chameleon, 1997)

The Straight Man – My Life In Comedy
by Nicholas Parsons (Weidenfeld & Nicolson, 1994)

Profiles by Kenneth Tynan
(Nick Hern Books, 1989)

British Television – An Illustrated Guide
compiled by Tise Vahimagi (Oxford University Press, 1994)

The Kenneth Williams Diaries
edited by Russell Davies (HarperCollins, 1993)

Still On My Way To Hollywood by Ernie Wise
with Trevor Barnes (Duckworth, 1990)

1 The Observer, 9 September 1973